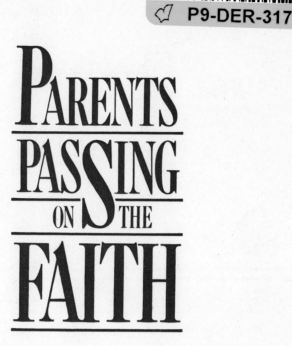

PARENTS PASSING ON THE FAITH

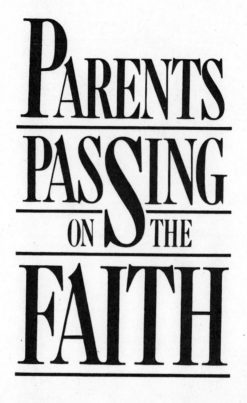

PARENTS PASSING ON THE FAITH

CARL K. SPACKMAN

VICTOR BOOKS®

A DIVISION OF SCRIPTURE PRESS PUBLICATIONS INC.
USA CANADA ENGLAND

Unless otherwise noted, Scripture quotations in this book are
from the *New American Standard Bible,* © The Lockman
Foundation 1960, 1962, 1963, 1968, 1971, 1972, 1973, 1975,
1977. Quotations marked KJV are taken from the *Authorized
(King James) Version.*

Recommended Dewey Decimal Classification: 248.8
Suggested Subject Heading: PERSONAL CHRISTIANITY
FOR PARENTS

Library of Congress Catalog Card Number: 89-60179
ISBN: 0-89693-753-4

TABLE OF CONTENTS

To Helen who has been my faithful partner in creating a sphere of godly influence in our home.

ACKNOWLEDGMENTS

This book is the result of the love and support of many friends who firmly believed in the value of its message for today's Christian community. I am deeply indebted to the elders and congregation of Maple Glen Bible Fellowship Church for their prayers, encouragement, and patience during the time of research and writing.

In particular, I want to thank the following three individuals:

Greg Gregoire, director of Student Venture in Philadelphia, who was instrumental in arranging for the circulation of my questionnaire at Youth Congress '85.

Lane Sattler, who spent hundreds of hours feeding the computer with facts from the 1,850 questionnaires and then helped me analyze all the data.

Murielle Withers, who read and reread the manuscript and offered invaluable suggestions.

Finally, I want to thank my wife, Helen, and my children, Brent, Laura, and Lynn, who "gave up" a husband and father for several months and did not let me lose confidence in myself when I was tempted to quit.

INTRODUCTION

If you are a Christian parent, or hope to be a parent someday, you no doubt have one deep-seated desire regarding
your children: you long to see them come to a vibrant and
growing personal relationship with the living God. Even
thinking about the possibility of one or more of your children rejecting the faith leaves you with a sick feeling in the
pit of your stomach. You may have observed the anguish of
other parents whose sons or daughters have rebelled and
gone the way of the world. Or you may have grown up in
the church yourself and watched some of your Sunday
School friends turn their backs on the faith. You know that
the cost of rejecting the faith is very high, both for those
who rebel and for their believing parents.

It is difficult to gather reliable statistics on the number
of young people raised in Christian homes who forsake the
faith, either temporarily or permanently; however, esti-
mates range from 50 percent to as high as 80 percent. Many
of these young people will return to the faith in later years,
but many others will not. In a September 1982 article in
Moody Monthly, Dennis Miller, president of Church Youth
Development Inc., explained, "Fifty percent of Christian

teenagers will sit in church next Sunday. Two years from now 70 percent of those who graduate from high school will leave and never come back."

Although they venture no similar statistical projections, other Christian leaders clearly share Miller's alarm. Of sixty pastors and full-time youth workers interviewed, fifty-six (93 percent) described the present phenomenon of faith rejection, the refusal of someone raised in a Christian home to be identified with the Christian faith, as either "fairly serious" or "extremely serious."

Indeed, the problem is too serious and too widespread to ignore. It crosses denominational, theological, cultural, and geographic barriers. Like a dreaded cancer, it quietly devastates the ranks of the church, inflicting grief upon Christian families and leading many to a certain spiritual death. Faith rejection is a problem of immense proportions that must be faced by both the church at large and parents in particular.

The purpose of this book is to assist young parents in developing child-rearing practices based on those principles which, if consistently practiced, will be most likely to lead their children to an enduring faith in Jesus Christ. These faith-formation principles are rooted in the teaching of the Bible. They have been selected after much research and serious thought concerning the subject of faith rejection. They are not new principles; they have been the basis of child-rearing practices used by many parents over the years. Their significance, however, has now been reinforced by the results of considerable investigation and study.

The content of this book is based largely on a survey I circulated at Youth Congress '85, held in Washington, D.C. in July of that year. Sponsored by Youth for Christ and Student Venture, this conference brought together more than 15,000 teenagers from the United States, Canada, and several other countries. Its major intent was to help Christian young people become more effective witnesses for

Christ on their high school campuses.

The eighty-five questions on the survey I distributed focused on the teen's relationship with God, his parents, and the church, as well as on the worldly pressures confronting the teenager of today. In particular, the survey was designed to discover the various factors, both general and specific, which contribute to the decision of our young people to reject the Christian faith.

Of approximately 12,000 questionnaires distributed, 1,850 were returned. The results were fed into a computer and became the primary source of information for this book. The accuracy and reliability of the data given by the Christian teens in the survey were confirmed by personal interviews with men and women who have denied the faith after being raised in Christian homes.

The question may fairly be asked, "Why did you investigate the problem of faith rejection by surveying Christian teenagers, especially those who, by their very presence at Youth Congress '85, were most likely to be seriously committed to the faith?" It is my conviction that very few young people raised in Christian homes pass through their teenage years without questioning to some degree the validity of the faith. It is part of the adolescent experience to challenge what adults believe and, in the process, develop one's own belief system. This means that teenagers raised in a Christian home will go through the process of analyzing what they have been taught and will either adopt it or reject it. In other words, I believe Christian young people are the most dependable source of information on faith rejection because not only have they considered the possibility of forsaking their parents' faith, but they have also struggled through the problems and found convincing reasons to adopt the faith as their own.

This is not so much a *how to* book as it is a *trust and obey* book. There are no surefire methods of raising our children so as to guarantee they will abide in the faith. The bottom line must always be the gracious, sovereign will of a loving God. He alone knows *how to* save our children. We are called upon to *obey* the faith-formation principles and precepts of His revealed Word and to *trust* Him to keep His promises.

We know from His dealings with mankind throughout history that God is a covenant-keeping God who draws His people primarily from the immediate generation of believers. That is, He delights in saving the children of believers. As Peter said on the Day of Pentecost, "For the promise [of the Spirit] is for you and your children." However, he also went on to say, "And for all who are afar off, as many as the Lord our God shall call to Himself" (Acts 2:39). God promises to include the children of believers within the scope of the blessings of salvation, but they are not brought into the faith automatically by virtue of their parents' faith. They must be called by God's Spirit through His Word, for "faith comes from hearing, and hearing by the Word of Christ" (Rom. 10:17).

This means our children must hear the Gospel. God has given us, as Christian parents, certain promises. He has also given us accompanying responsibilities. We are entrusted with the stewardship of each child He gives to us— a stewardship which involves bringing them, through our words and actions, into the path of faith. It is my desire that the material in this book will be a valuable tool for helping parents fulfill this God-given stewardship as they seek to lead their children to an enduring faith in Him.

CHAPTER ONE

BEGIN WITH A CLEAR VIEW

Faith-formation Principle: To help our children come to an enduring faith in Christ, we must begin the parenting process with a clear view of their spiritual nature at birth. We must also have a clear view of the final goal of the parenting process as it relates to our children's ultimate spiritual condition.

Biblical Text: Proverbs 16:9
Parenting is unfamiliar territory for most couples. Even though it is probably the most significant responsibility they will ever assume in life, many parents approach the task with minimal training. For Christian couples the task of raising a family involves the even greater challenge of leading children into a personal relationship with Jesus Christ.

Understandably, the thoughts of entering this new domain of parenting can be a little intimidating for couples who take seriously their God-given stewardship. Not only are they assuming responsibility for their child's physical and emotional well-being, but they are also becoming directly involved in the care of his soul. Where do new par-

ents look for direction as they begin to travel through this
unknown territory? The obvious place to begin is with the
familiar landmarks that God Himself has provided in His
Word.

As a young man of eighteen I learned the importance of
trusting in available guideposts. My three friends and I had
just watched our hockey team win an exciting game on the
opponent's home ice. As we left the arena to drive twenty-
seven miles home, a light snow was falling. Within minutes,
however, the weather changed drastically. I was soon driving through the worst blizzard I had ever been in. To make
the situation even more frightening, it was near midnight
and bitterly cold. Fortunately, I had been on this highway
many times before, so even though my view of the road
ahead was almost nil, I was basically familiar with the
turns and bridges and hills. Still, the only way we could
navigate was to creep along at 10–20 miles an hour and
keep our heads out the windows to see how close we were
to the telephone poles that lined the road. They were our
only guideposts that night. Several times we veered off the
road into the ditch or across the road into the opposite
lane. But the Lord got us safely home. What was generally
a thirty-minute drive took three hours.

This personal experience illustrates what I believe is one
of the initial problems facing young parents who desire to
lead their children safely into the faith. They do not have a
clear view of the road ahead. In fact, some parents are not
even sure where they are going. They may start out on the
parenting journey with romantic ideas about being able to
coast along with the greatest of ease, only to discover
when the blizzard strikes that they really aren't as familiar
with the surroundings as they thought they were. If they
know the guideposts along the way—the faith-formation
principles—they have a much better chance of staying on
course and getting their passengers safely to their des-
tination.

In Proverbs 16:9 we read, "The mind of man plans his

way, but the LORD directs his steps." Solomon brings
together in this one verse the two truths that seem so
irreconcilable to human understanding—namely, the sovereignty of God and the freedom and responsibility of man.
Man proposes but God disposes. These are the two lenses
through which we must view all of life, including what
happens to our children. For instance, if we look at our
children only through the lens of human responsibility, we
will have a distorted image of reality. We will think that
their well-being and final end depends entirely on us, their
parents. If our children happen to end up rejecting the
faith, we are devastated and overwhelmed with guilt because we feel we are responsible. On more than one occasion I have had hurting parents in my study asking the
question, "Where did we go wrong? What could we have
done to keep our child in the faith?" They feel that somehow they are the cause of their child's rebellion.

On the other hand, if we look at our children only
through the lens of God's sovereignty, we will have an
equally distorted view of them. We will be tempted to sit
back and say, "God is in control of all things including
whether or not my children will come to faith in Christ.
There is nothing I can do except pray for them." If our
children then turn away from the faith, we won't blame
ourselves because we believe He directs our steps and
theirs. But we may end up blaming God. Instead of saying,
"Where did I go wrong?" we may say, "Why me, God? I
didn't deserve this burden."

The fact is, both parts of Solomon's proverb are true, and
we must believe and act on both elements if we are to have
a biblical view of reality in general and of our parenting
roles in particular. Christian parents must be willing to
acknowledge the truth of the words: "In Him also we have
obtained an inheritance, having been predestined according to His purpose who works all things after the counsel
of His will" (Eph. 1:10-11). He saves whom He wills (Rom.
9:15-16); however, this does not mean we approach

parenting with a spirit of fatalism, reluctantly resigned to whatever God has determined regarding the salvation of our children. Solomon's counsel is: "The mind of man plans his way" or, as he says in Proverbs 16:1, "The plans of the heart belong to man." God expects us, as parents, to plan how we are going to raise our children—how we are going to lead them to an enduring faith in Christ. More than that, He promises to bless our plans if they are in accord with biblical guidelines. To that end He has included our children in the promise of salvation (Acts 2:39). But their salvation will not happen without faithful instruction in the Word of God by parents (2 Tim. 3:14-17) and consistent modeling of the faith in the home (2 Tim. 1:5).

In other words, we must begin our parenting responsibilities with a firm trust in God's gracious will but also with a plan. We must know both where we want to take our children and the best road to get them there. The more familiar we are with the guideposts along the way and the more closely we follow them, the more confident we can be that God will see us safely through to the end of the road. We can then face the storms and blizzards of life, which are sure to come in the course of the child-rearing process, with the confidence that He is in full control of whatever happens.

When I set out for home that late, wintry night, I knew exactly where I was going and the best road to get there. I was well acquainted with the guideposts along the way, and I trusted them. But ultimately my peace was based on the fact that I knew God loved me and that He was in full control. Even though I found the storm to be somewhat intimidating, I was able to persevere with the full confidence that if I stayed on the road as best I could, He would bring my friends and me home safely.

It is that same kind of confidence which believing parents can have as they commence the awesome task of training their children in the faith. Leading our sons and daughters to their Heavenly Father can be a joyful and rewarding task. But we must have a plan. We must begin with a clear view of two specific facts: (1) the spiritual condition of our children as they begin life's journey, and (2) the goal of the parenting process as it relates to the spiritual condition of our children.

MAINTAIN A CLEAR VIEW OF
YOUR CHILD'S SPIRITUAL CONDITION AT BIRTH

Christians do not all agree on the subject of the spiritual condition of children at the time of their birth. Many are not even sure what they believe regarding the spiritual nature of their infants. This difference of opinion and general ignorance on the part of parents complicates their understanding of the problem of faith rejection and their ability to find a solution for it. Because they do not have a clear view of the nature of their children, they cannot set a clear course for training them.

Historically, there have been basically three different ways of viewing the spiritual state of infants. We will call them:

(1) Saved Children
(2) Covenant Children
(3) Unbelieving Children

Saved Children

Many Christians believe that when God made His covenant with Abraham and his descendants, He was assuring believing parents that their children would be included in the promised blessings of salvation (Gen. 17:7). Proponents of this view speak of the covenant blessings flowing in "the line of generations." To demonstrate their confidence in this promise to their children, they baptize children as a sign and seal of the covenant God first made with Abraham.

Some of these Christians, however, conclude that the covenant promise also gives them the right to view their children as regenerate or spiritually alive at birth. This view has been called "presupposed" or "presumptive" regeneration. Adherents of this view approach the training of their children with the assumption that since they already have a regenerate heart, they will automatically believe in Christ. The implication is that their children, unlike the children of unbelievers, do not need to be told of their sinful natures (Prov. 22:15; Ps. 51:5; Rom. 5:12) or encouraged to repent and believe the Gospel; they will do it naturally.

Although this view is not as popular as it once was, some believers still hold to it. I had one man tell me that because he believed his daughters were born with regenerate hearts, they should be taught and treated as Christians. He fully expected them to act as Christians from the time of their infancy.

Covenant Children

The majority of those who baptize their children as a sign and seal of God's covenant promise do not presume their children to be regenerate at birth. Instead, they speak of them as covenant children who are to be viewed as members of the visible church. As such, they are to be given all the rights and privileges of fellowship associated with the body of Christ.

Even though parents who hold to this view would readily acknowledge their children's sinful nature and need for conversion once they reach the age of discernment, these parents are constantly faced with the temptation to treat their children as if they were already regenerate. Because children are looked upon as organically united to the *visible* body of Christ by virtue of their birth into a Christian home, some parents may begin to assume that they are also a part of the *invisible* church. But to carelessly slip into regarding them as almost in the kingdom is to ignore the fact that covenant children also need to be taught the whole counsel of God, including the essentials of the Gospel. Not to do so is to deny them the very means by which

God promises to fulfill His covenant obligations (2 Tim. 3:14-17). My own children attended a Christian school where several of the teachers seemed to treat all the students as believers. The teachers assumed that because these children came from believing families, they would have a heart to understand spiritual truth and would behave as little believers.

Unbelieving Children

The third view is generally maintained by Baptists and those Christians who hold to believer's baptism by immersion. It is the conviction that guided my parents. They did not view my brother and me as regenerate at birth or members of the covenant, the kingdom of heaven, or the visible church. Rather, beginning with the doctrine of original sin, they believed we were born with sinful natures and under the penalty of death (Rom. 5:12). They, therefore, were convinced that we needed to be confronted with the Gospel and urged to personally repent and believe in Jesus Christ.

I can remember as a child of six or seven sitting on benches in our kitchen, with a dozen other neighborhood children, as the Child Evangelism worker presented the Gospel message to us. Week after week, by means of flannelgraph stories and flash cards, she would tell us about our sin and our need to trust in Jesus for forgiveness of that sin. Great stress was laid upon each child asking Jesus to come into his heart. My parents believed that membership in the covenant, in the kingdom of heaven, and in the invisible church depended on each of us making a personal confession of faith.

Unfortunately, some who hold to this third viewpoint overlook something which adherents to the other two positions correctly regard as crucial. They ignore the special position that children of believers have in the eyes of God. In essence, they view the children of believers as no different from the children of unbelievers. This, I believe, is wrong and harmful. It is wrong because, despite our different interpretations of specific passages of God's Word, we cannot deny the fact that God has placed children of believers in a unique situation. Paul says they are "holy" or "sanctified" by the believing parent (1 Cor. 7:14). Whatever the apostle intends by his use of the word *holy*, he certainly means that children of believers are set apart from the children of unbelievers. At the very least, he is suggesting that by virtue of their Christian heritage they have been placed in the pathway of faith or within the sphere of Gospel influence. If God still saves His people primarily through the line of generations, and I believe He does, then our children are in a special position with both unique privileges and unique responsibilities. This fact alone ought to encourage us as we seek to instruct our children in the faith.

The following illustration depicts the three different views of the spiritual status of believers' children at birth. The large figures represent the believing parents and the small figures represent their children.

1. Saved Children

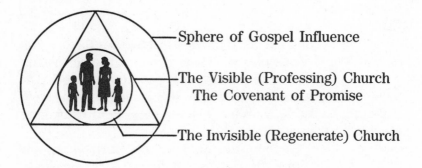

Children of believing parents are viewed as in the sphere of Gospel influence, the visible and the invisible church, and the covenant of promise.

2. Covenant Children

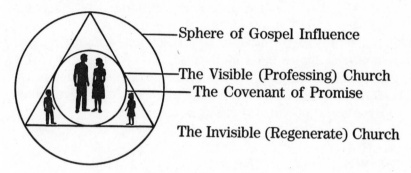

Sphere of Gospel Influence

The Visible (Professing) Church
The Covenant of Promise

The Invisible (Regenerate) Church

Children of believing parents are viewed as in the sphere of Gospel influence, the visible church, and the covenant of promise, but not the invisible church.

3. Unbelieving Children

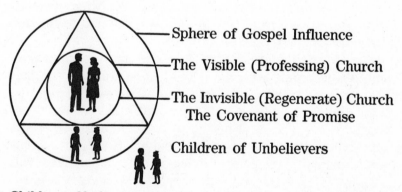

Sphere of Gospel Influence

The Visible (Professing) Church

The Invisible (Regenerate) Church
The Covenant of Promise

Children of Unbelievers

Children of believing parents are viewed as in the sphere of Gospel influence but not as in the church visible or invisible. Baptists identify the moment of birth into the invisible church as the time when one receives the promised blessings of the covenant. The children of unbelievers, unless raised by believers, are even outside the sphere of Gospel influence.

Perhaps by now you are asking yourself, "Why must I

have a clear view of the spiritual nature of my children at birth? Why can't I just accept my children as gifts from God and trust Him to help me to make the right decisions at the right time? Why must I go through the mental agony of trying to figure out which of the three viewpoints is the correct one?" Hopefully the answer to these questions will emerge as we look briefly at the importance of developing a clear view of our parenting goals.

MAINTAIN A CLEAR VIEW
OF YOUR PARENTING GOALS

We must understand the basic spiritual nature of our children at birth, but we must also have a clear picture in mind of the spiritual nature we want to see in them ultimately. As Christian parents, we not only want our children to develop into mature adults who can function on their own, but we also long for them to come to faith in Christ and grow up as Christian decision-makers. We want them to look at all of life from God's point of view and to live for His glory.

The Apostle Paul told the Colossians that he admonished and taught people with the goal of presenting "every man complete in Christ" (Col. 1:28). Surely, we cannot improve on that as a goal in the training of our children. We must, therefore, know what it means to be "complete in Christ," and then we must begin to lead our children toward that goal. Obviously, we can only begin the process. They will not always be under our authority. But while they are, we cannot just sit back and hope everything will fall into place simply because our children are within the sphere of Gospel influence. We must "plan our way," as Solomon puts it. In other words, we must familiarize ourselves with the guideposts of the faith-formation principles that God has established to help us lead our children to faith in Him.

Perhaps the most important principle of all is that God Himself is most likely to work in the lives of our children in order to make them complete in Christ. Archibald Alexander, writing on the subject of early childhood piety, says: "The education of children should proceed on the principle that they are in an unregenerate state, until evidences of piety clearly appear, in which case they should be sedulously cherished and nurtured."[1]

Alexander's comment touches on a critical point. Our understanding of the spiritual condition of our children directly influences our approach to their education in the faith. As one who holds to the second position discussed earlier, Alexander believes we must view our children as unregenerate.until we see evidence of God's regenerating work of grace in their hearts. As an adherent to position three, I would heartily agree with him. If we regard our children as unregenerate and in need of saving faith, we are going to seek to weave the Gospel into our instruction of them. We are going to have to be evangelists within the home.

Dr. Jay Adams, in his book *Back to the Blackboard*, suggests that parents should be supported in this task by the Christian school teacher. He writes:

> Every teacher in a school should conceive of himself as a parental evangelist. Because we do not ever know finally who is and who is not a Christian, it is important to keep the Gospel before the student body at all stages throughout their entire time at school.[2]

Parents, are you prepared to "do the work of an evangelist" (2 Tim. 4:5) within your own home? Those who hold to the first viewpoint will not feel the need to pursue this particular course because they already presuppose their children's salvation. Those of us who identify with either position two or three, however, will want to know how to best communicate the Gospel to our children.

But, does believing in the need to evangelize our children mean we treat them as sinful degenerates who are no different from the children of unbelieving pagans? Of course not. Does it mean we expect our children to come to faith the exact same way unbelievers do? No, not necessarily.

Unbelievers, not raised in a Christian home, generally come to accept the faith through a process that involves the hearing of the Gospel, conviction of sin, and an intelligent embracing of Christ through faith and repentance. We call this conversion to the Christian faith. Usually, the convert is aware of a specific moment in his or her life when this transference from the kingdom of darkness to the kingdom of light occurred.

This, however, is not the general pattern for the conversion of children raised in Christian homes. Granted, some approaches to child evangelism do tend to stress a one-time experience in which children are urged to pray to receive Jesus. Parents may even put pressure upon their children to "make a decision." But, even though God is pleased to use this approach to lead some children into the kingdom, it does not usually happen that way in Christian homes.

Children who have been raised within the sphere of Gospel influence have been exposed to the Word of God and a Christian environment throughout their entire childhood. It is natural, therefore, for children of believers to experience from time to time what Archibald Alexander calls "early religious impressions." These are common operations of the Spirit which result in such responses as feelings of guilt over a sinful act or deep sorrow over disobedience to one's parents. They may also create in our children a fear of dying and going to hell or a sense of joy and love for Jesus. They may be very intense feelings at the time, but they do not last. Indeed, they may be forgotten entirely within days. But these experiences ought not to be taken lightly. They may very well have a cumulative effect within the minds of our children. Like the adding of more and more coals to a smoldering fire, these early religious impressions can, in God's good and perfect time, ultimately provide the fuel for conversion and burst into a full-blown flame of faith and repentance.

In all of this we must recognize that salvation is entirely of the Lord for, "Unless the Lord build the house, they labor in vain who build it" (Ps. 127:1). Even though we are responsible to "plan our way" by getting as clear a view as possible of the spiritual nature of our children and of our parenting goals, we must willingly commit our children and all our parenting efforts to the Lord who "directs our steps." We must keep our eyes on the markers He has given in His Word to guide us, but all the while be trusting Him to help us lead our children safely through the storms of life to an abiding rest in Him.

I have left unsaid much about the spiritual nature of our children and the goal and methods of the parenting process, but I hope our brief discussion has at least challenged parents to begin developing a clearer view in these important areas. The questions that follow are designed to stimulate further thought and discussion regarding some of the issues considered in this chapter.

For Review, Discussion, and Action:

1. With which view of a child's spiritual nature at birth do you identify? Why?

2. What are the potential dangers of each of the three positions?

3. Since adherents to positions two and three view their children as unregenerate until they see evidence of new life, how should they treat them prior to that evidence—as Christians or as non-Christians? Illustrate your answer with specific examples.

4. In what sense do you view your children as "holy"? (See 1 Cor. 7:14.)

5. The Apostle Paul, in Colossians 1:28, speaks about "presenting every man complete in Christ." How do you plan to do this with your own children?

6. In the chapter, mention was made of "early religious impressions" and the "common operations of the Holy Spirit" in the lives of our children. Do you agree that these experiences occur? What evidence from the lives of your own children leads you to this conclusion?

For Further Study:

Hanko, Herman. *We and Our Children.* Grand Rapids: Reformed Free Publishing Association, 1981. This book was written in response to David Kingdon's *Children of Abraham* by a man who identifies with the second view, that we should regard our children as members of the visible church.

Hoeksema, Herman. *Believers and Their Seed.* Grand Rapids: Reformed Free Publishing Association, 1971. Hoeksema, who holds to the second view, gives a critique of Abraham Kuyper who championed view one.

Inchley, John. *Kids and the Kingdom.* Wheaton: Tyndale House Publishers, Inc., 1976. This is a helpful little book written by a man who seems to waver between viewpoints number one and two.

Kingdon, David. *Children of Abraham.* Sussex: Carey Publications Ltd., 1973. Kingdon, a Baptist, argues for view number three, that we should regard our children as unregenerate until we see evidence that they have been born again.

CHAPTER TWO

TRAIN THEM EARLY AND INDIVIDUALLY

Faith-formation Principle: *To help our children come to an enduring faith in Christ, we must initiate them into the Christian faith at an early age. We must also treat them as individuals uniquely created by God for His glory.*

Biblical Text: Proverbs 22:6

One day early in my ministry a couple came to my study distraught over the struggles they were having with their oldest child, a fourteen-year-old daughter. She was resisting their authority in the home and refusing to go to church or youth group—showing evidence of a spirit of rebellion against the Christian faith in general. As I talked with these parents, I discovered that they had only been Christians for a few years. Since their conversion, they had tried to raise their children in accordance with biblical principles, and they seemed to be doing a fair job with their younger children. But the oldest daughter would not accept this new way of thinking and living.

"I really don't understand why she is fighting our authority," the mother said. "We have always tried to treat our children exactly the same way. We teach them the same way, discipline them the same way, love them the same way, and expect the same kind of response from them. Why is our oldest child rebelling against us so much?"

The answer to her question involved a number of inter-related factors, of course, but two things stood out immediately in our first session: (1) the parents had not started to train their oldest daughter in the Christian faith early enough, and (2) they had failed to deal with her, indeed with all their children, as individuals. In this chapter we will focus our thinking on these two important parental responsibilities.

TRAIN THEM FOR THE FUTURE

Our text, Proverbs 22:6, is a much-quoted verse that has been used by hurting Christian parents as a source of comfort when one of their children rebels against the faith. Unfortunately, Proverbs 22:6 is misinterpreted by many Christians. In fact, the common interpretation of the verse is actually directly the opposite of what Solomon is really saying.

Solomon states: "Train up a child in the way he should go, even when he is old he will not depart from it." Most of us who were raised in an evangelical church have been told that this verse means parents who train their children in the Word of God can have the assurance that, even if those children reject the faith during their teenage years, they will return to the fold when they get older. But when Solomon says, "even when he is old he will not depart from it," he is not giving us a sure promise that our children will accept the faith in their old age despite how they live in their youth. He is not suggesting that even if they reject the faith when they are young, sowing their wild oats and wasting many years, God will make all that training "click" when they are old and ready to die, and they will return to the faith.

This does not mean, of course, that God never deals with

the unrepentant children of believers in later years by drawing them back to the faith in which they had been trained. Praise God, He is a merciful and compassionate Father. He does save some children of believers "when they are old." I remember hearing the story years ago of the famous sixteenth-century slave trader, John Newton. In the midst of a violent storm, he called out to God for mercy, and God spared his life. Whole passages of Scripture, which Newton had learned years before on his mother's knee, flooded the drowning sailor's mind and guided him back to the shelter of the faith in which he had been trained. The Lord spared his life, and Newton went on to be a godly pastor and author of such hymns as "Amazing Grace" and "How Sweet the Name of Jesus Sounds." God can and does restore some prodigal sons and daughters to the faith. But that is not what Solomon is implying here.

What he is suggesting is that the way our children are trained now seriously affects the direction of their entire lives; indeed, the training sets them in a certain way that will prevail even when they are old. The word *old* means, literally, "hair on the chin" or "bearded one." Hence, it refers to a young man who has reached maturity. The word is not referring to someone who has lived his life in separation from God only to return to the faith in his years of retirement. The implication of the text is that by the time our children are old, i.e., mature young people, they will be fairly well set in their ways.

A German proverb says, "What little *Johnnie* does not learn, *John* learns never." A similar English saying suggests, "Just as the twig is bent, the tree is inclined." Solomon's proverb includes the same thrust. Our training determines the particular bent of our children, a bent that will remain with them even when they reach maturity. That is precisely what happened with the fourteen-year-old in the opening illustration of this chapter. Her parents had trained her a certain way during her childhood so that her particular bent, by the time they became Christians, was in a direction opposed to the faith. It did not mean God was powerless to change her heart and bend her in a new direction just as He had done with her parents, but the fact remained that she was inclined in a direction away from Christianity because that is how she had been trained since birth.

BEGIN TRAINING EARLY

Parents must never underestimate the importance of initiating their children in the faith right from the beginning of their lives. Solomon implies this by the use of the word *train.* It has a very interesting meaning in the original language. It comes from a Hebrew root word meaning, "to put in the mouth" or "to affect the taste." The equivalent Arabic word was used to describe the action of the nurse or the mother putting date syrup on the palate of a newborn to stimulate sucking, developing a child's desire for his mother's breast. Gradually the word came to mean "to initiate," then "to dedicate" and finally "to catechize" or "to train."

To the Hebrew people, beginnings were very important. For example, in Deuteronomy 20:5-7, Moses sets forth three reasons for military exemption: (1) A man has built a new home and needs to dedicate it, which most commentators suggest meant inviting his friends and family over for an extensive time of feasting and celebration; (2) A man has planted a vineyard but has not enjoyed the firstfruits of it yet; (3) A man has just been married and needs to start a family. In each case, the men were initiating something new or dedicating it for its proper use. The home was a place to show hospitality; the fruit of a vineyard was for enjoying; marriage was for raising offspring.

The word *train* contains the same idea. It has to do with initiating or inaugurating our children in the direction they should go. We don't wait until they reach school age before we start dealing with them from a Christian perspective. As the Apostle Paul commands us in Ephesians 6:4, we should begin immediately to "bring them up in the discipline and instruction of the Lord." That is why it is so important for us as parents to have a clear view of our children's spiritual condition at birth: our training of them must begin early. Psychologists tell us children can begin developing inclinations toward certain things even in the womb. So some expectant mothers tune a radio to classical music and plop it on their tummy. Others read to their unborn child. Whether or not the reading of God's Word or the playing of Christian music will have any positive effect on our unborn children is highly questionable. What it does do, however, is create an environment very early in their lives which is preparatory for their entrance into the sphere of Gospel influence.

In 2 Timothy 3:15 Paul tells Timothy that, "from childhood [literally 'infancy'] you have known the sacred writings which are able to give you the wisdom that leads to salvation through faith which is in Christ Jesus." Lois and Eunice initiated Timothy in the Scriptures while he was still in diapers. They didn't wait until they were sure he understood everything he was taught or until he reached some mysterious age of accountability. They knew that Timothy was accountable to God the moment he was born and that if he were to receive "the wisdom that leads to salvation," he would have to be taught the sacred writings of the Scriptures. He would have to "learn" and "become convinced of" them (2 Tim. 3:14). So they began his training early.

What Solomon is saying in Proverbs 22:6, then, is that just as that date gum creates a thirst in the infant's mouth and initiates the impulse for sucking, so also we, as parents, are to initiate in our children early in life a tendency to go in a certain direction. We cannot leave them on their own for the first few years and hope they will automatically adopt the Christian way. By nature, they will be no more inclined to hunger for the Word of God than they will be to crave the most nourishing physical food. They must be taught what is best for them in both the physical and the spiritual realms. If we do not become involved in the early training of our children, they will be more likely to follow the world's way and ultimately rebel against the faith itself.

The Book of Proverbs also stresses this need for early training in terms of the discipline of our children. Proverbs 19:18 reminds us: "Discipline your son while there is hope and do not desire his death." The implication is, if you don't discipline him early in life, there will be no hope of successfully disciplining him later. He will already be bent in the wrong direction.

If we want our children to hunger after righteousness and to seek first the kingdom of God, then Solomon says we must first of all initiate them early in the Christian faith. We must prepare the mold, whet the appetite, set the course, and begin to train them in the direction we believe God would have them go. But what is the direction in which we should lead our kids? Well, you say, we should lead them in the direction of the Christian faith. We should lead them to Christ. Yes, of course we should. But again, Proverbs 22:6 may be giving us a somewhat different idea.

INDIVIDUALIZE THE TRAINING
Solomon says: "Train up a child in the way he should go." The expression, "the way he should go" may be understood in several different ways.

(1) It has been generally interpreted in a moral sense to mean "train your children in the Christian way; that's the way they should go." That certainly is a legitimate understanding of the text; however, the Hebrew expression itself is not restricted to this one meaning.

(2) It may also be translated, "in the way he *would* go" meaning, "the way he would go if left to his own sinful nature." The idea here is that if we train our children in accordance with their sinful natures, allowing them to do basically as they please, that's exactly what they will do. In fact, even when they are old they will still be doing what

comes naturally. This too is a legitimate interpretation.

(3) I believe, however, that the third possible interpretation is the best one. The expression, "in the way he should go" means literally, as the marginal reference in the NASB puts it, "according to his way." Commentators Keil and Delitzsch translate it, "conformable to his way." In other words, "Train up a child according to, or in conformity with, his way." But what does that mean? It could mean either of the following:

(a) "in conformity with his abilities as a child."

This interpretation would make the developmental child psychologists and child educators happy. It suggests that parents should adapt the training of their children to the particular abilities and interests of the children at each stage of their development. Although this is an excellent educational principle, I do not believe it is what Solomon had in mind.

(b) "in conformity with the child's unique nature and distinctive qualities."

The word *way* in the Hebrew suggests the idea of "manner," "mode," or "characteristic." In Psalm 7:12 and Psalm 11:2 it is used to describe a bow being bent. In Proverbs 30:18-19 we read:

> There are three things which are too wonderful for me, four which I do not understand: the *way* of an eagle in the sky, the *way* of a serpent on a rock, the *way* of a ship in the middle of the sea, and the *way* of a man with a maid (emphasis added).

The author uses the word *way* to describe the general characteristic or natural bent of each of the four subjects. They each act a certain way in their own environment because of their distinctive natures. Similarly, each of our children possess their own unique natures. That's what Solomon seems to be implying in Proverbs 22:6.

Barnes defines "in the way he should go," as:

according to the tenor of his way, i.e., the pattern
specially belonging to, specially fitted for the individual's character. The proverb enjoins the closest
possible study of each child's temperament and the
adaptation of his way of life to that.

Everyone who has more than one child knows that God
has made each of them out of separate molds. They each
have a different personality, temperament, talents,
strengths, weaknesses, etc. They are "bent" differently. But
do we treat them as such? Do we *individualize* our training of them so that they know we care for them and try to
understand them as individual persons? I'm not saying we
should forget about establishing common standards or
rules which apply to all children equally. Of course we
must have certain ground rules that apply to all family
members alike; however, we cannot ignore the distinctive
gifts and qualities that God has given each of our children.
To do so is to court disaster.

One teenage girl said, "I have to be myself. I can't be
anyone else or act like anyone else. I just have to be me."
And I think she speaks for most teens. Despite their tendency to want to be like their peers in certain things—
dress, morals, hairstyles, etc. (the more external things),
they still have an internal, unique, God-given individuality
that cries out for recognition.

FOLLOW GOD'S EXAMPLE

The importance of treating our children as individuals is
implied not only by the fact that God has created them
with unique abilities and personalities but also by the fact
that in the new creation He renews them individually. This
was not always God's primary way of dealing with His
people. In the Old Testament period, He followed the principle of representative headship—the father or the head of
the clan acted on behalf of those under him. In other
words, the welfare of the family depended upon the obedi-

ence (Ex. 12:3, 23) or disobedience (Josh. 7:24-25) of the father.

In the second commandment the Lord indicated that His judgment for the sins of one generation would be vented on succeeding generations (Ex. 20:5-6). This did not mean individuals of each generation escaped responsibility for their own sinful conduct (Deut. 24:16), but it did mean that God would administer either blessing or cursing on other people (namely, succeeding generations) because of the sins of others.

It is significant that one of the characteristics of the New Covenant, predicted by Jeremiah, is that there would be no doubt whatsoever in the coming age as to the individual responsibility of every person for his/her own sin (Jer. 31:29-30). The Jews had used the proverb, "The fathers eat the sour grapes, but the children's teeth are set on edge" (Ezek. 18:2-4), to charge God with injustice and cruelty for punishing children for the sins of their fathers. The prophet Jeremiah, however, makes it clear that the days are coming when, "everyone will die for his own iniquity; each man who eats the sour grapes, his teeth shall be set on edge" (Jer. 31:30). The prophet Ezekiel not only agrees with Jeremiah when he says, "the soul who sins shall die" (Ezek. 18:4), but he gives a detailed illustration of how the principle of personal responsibility for sin works in the line of generations (Ezek. 18:5-17).

The prophets are clearly pointing ahead to the new age that would be ushered in at the coming of Christ. At that time the old Mosaic Covenant would give way to the New Covenant with its emphasis upon the work of God in the hearts of individuals. The Lord promised that at that time He would put His law "within them" and write it "on their heart" (Jer. 31:33 and Ezek. 36:25-27). The result of this inward cleansing and renewing work would be that "they shall all know Me, from the least of them to the greatest of them" (Jer. 31:34). God may still work through family or generational lines to save His people, but the emphasis in the New Testament age is clearly upon His gracious work in the lives of individuals. The principle of headship is fulfilled in Jesus Christ, the true seed of Abraham (Gal. 3:16). Those who desire membership in the family of faith must individually put their trust in Him alone.

Clearly, God knows and deals with each of our children as individuals. He made them as unique persons and when, by His grace, He determines to draw them to Himself, He deals with them again as special individuals. He knows exactly how to bring each of our children under conviction of sin, how to interest them in the Gospel, and how to motivate them to confess faith in Christ. He knows how each of them can best grow in the faith and what form of discipline will be most effective when they stray.

How well do you know your children? In 1 Peter 3:7 the Lord directs husbands to deal with their wives in an "understanding way." The word means literally, "according to knowledge." In other words, husbands must work hard at getting to know everything they can about their wives and then treat them in accordance with that knowledge. That is what I believe Solomon is saying in Proverbs 22:6. He is implying that we should get to know our children as the individuals God made them to be and treat them as such.

You who have children—are you really striving to understand them as individuals and to deal with them accordingly? Or are you like the mother mentioned in the opening illustration? You have a certain game plan that you are determined to follow no matter how different your children may be from each other. You force each of them into this common mold despite how much they keep oozing out over the sides. Do you discipline each child exactly the same way or, perhaps I should say, to the same extent, even though one child may be much more sensitive and more responsive to your discipline than another? If you do, you may be headed for trouble somewhere down the road.

Proverbs 22:6 encourages us to initiate our children in the Christian doctrine and way of life early in their lives and to treat them as individuals uniquely created by God. We must get to know each of them as thoroughly as we can so that we can use the most effective methods to lead them to an enduring faith in Christ.

For Review, Discussion, and Action:

1. What was the original meaning of the words *to train* in Proverbs 22:6? What implications does that meaning have for parents trying to raise their children in the faith?

2. What are three different ways of interpreting the words, "in the way he should go" in Proverbs 22:6? What is the original meaning of the word *way*?

3. What are some positive and negative effects of treating our children as individuals?

4. How are you presently expressing to your children that they are special individuals in your sight? Give specific examples.

5. If Proverbs 22:6 cannot be properly used as a source of comfort for believing parents whose child has forsaken the faith, what verses or scriptural truths could be a source of encouragement?

For Further Study:

Adams, Jay E. *Back to the Blackboard.* Phillipsburg: Presbyterian and Reformed Publishing Company, 1982. This book proposes a radical revision of our present approach to Christian education. It is based on the assumption that God has created our children as individuals and therefore our methodologies ought to help each child reach his or her maximum potential in service for Christ.

Greenfield, Guy. *The Wounded Parent.* Grand Rapids: Baker Book House, 1982. A pastor and seminary professor offers advice on how to handle the many painful emotions and problems that accompany the loss of a child to the world's value system.

Lewis, Margie M. *The Hurting Parent.* Grand Rapids: Zondervan Publishing House, 1980. A moving account of how one family dealt with the pain of a son who, for a time, turned his back on the faith.

Swindoll, Charles R. *You and Your Child.* Nashville: Thomas Nelson Inc., Publishers 1977. Swindoll goes into considerable detail in his interpretation and application of Proverbs 22:6.

White, John. *Parents in Pain.* Downers Grove: InterVarsity Press, 1979. One of the best books thus far on coping with the trauma of faith rejection by one of your children.

CHAPTER THREE

INCULCATE AND INOCULATE

Faith-formation Principle: *To help our children come to an enduring faith in Christ we must, in every possible way, inculcate them with the truth of God's Word. As part of this inculcation, we must repeatedly inoculate them against the man-centered philosophies and godless lifestyles of the world.*

Biblical Text: Deuteronomy 6:4-9
In the introduction to this book I referred to a questionnaire which I distributed at the Washington D.C. Youth Congress in July 1985. The survey dealt with factors in teens' homes, churches, and personal lives that may or may not affect their attitude toward the Christian faith. Over 97 percent of the 1,850 individuals participating in the survey professed to be Christians. In fact, many of the teens were at Youth Congress '85 because of their deep commitment to Christ and their desire to reach fellow students for Him. I assumed, however, that many of those who had been raised in Christian homes had struggled with the issue of rejecting the faith. Indeed, 35 percent said they had considered rejecting the faith, and 39 percent claimed that they

had rejected it for a while.

At the end of the questionnaire, I listed twelve possible reasons children raised in Christian homes might have for rejecting Christianity. I asked the young people to indicate which of the twelve reasons listed (or other reasons not listed) would most likely contribute to a decision to reject the faith. They were then asked to identify which of the twelve reasons would be the *most* compelling. In the following table I have ranked the young people's response to that question.

Most Compelling Reason to Reject the Faith	*Percent*
(1) The appeal of worldly attractions	20.5
(2) Hypocrites in the church	19.3
(3) Peer pressure from unbelievers	13.7
(4) A strong attachment to non-Christian friends	11.4
(5) Poor Christian role models in my home	7.9
(6) Other reasons	5.7
(7) Christian adults don't listen, they lecture	5.1
(8) Can always become a Christian later in life	4.9
(9) Ashamed of being identified as a Christian	4.0
(10) Too many doubts about the Bible	3.8
(11) Christianity has too many rules	1.6
(12) Christianity doesn't relate to my life	1.2
(13) Difficulty in believing Christ is the only way	0.9

With 57.5 percent of the young people identifying it as a potential cause of faith rejection and 20.5 percent saying it would be for them the most compelling reason, the number one reason for faith rejection is clearly "the attraction of the world." A close second is "hypocrites in the church," with "peer pressure" and "a strong attachment to non-Christian friends" ranking as the third and fourth reasons.

It would appear, from a cursory view of the top four reasons for faith rejection, that youth raised in Christian homes today are caught in a tremendous struggle with the pressures of the world and those who identify with it. Be-

cause this is such a crucial area of concern for the subject
of faith rejection, we will consider it in this chapter and the
next one. In the next chapter we will focus on the need for
children (and their parents) to develop a biblical view of
the world and worldliness.

In this chapter we are going to look at two indispens-
able, foundational truths for helping our children develop a
Christian approach to life. The primary truth—the need to
inculcate in our children the teachings of God's Word—
was first given to Moses and to the people of Israel when
they were about to go into the Promised Land. It was
meant to help prepare them and the next generation to
remain true to the revealed faith when they were confronted with all the evil enticements of the Canaanite nations.
The second truth we will look at—the need to inoculate
our children against the "diseases" of the world—is a natural outgrowth of the first truth. It is not so much commanded in the Scriptures as it is implied by the biblical teaching
on the world and how Christians are to live in it.

INCULCATE WITH THE
TRUTH IN EVERY POSSIBLE WAY

The word *inculcate* means, "to impress by repeated statement or admonition; to teach persistently and earnestly"
(*The American College Dictionary*). It means more than
"indoctrinate"; it involves the use of varied methods of
instruction in order to impress the truth on our children.

Deuteronomy 6:4-9 is the key passage here. As mentioned above, the Lord is preparing His people to enter the
Promised Land (v. 1). Moses specifically states in verse 2
that these commandments were for the present generation,
its sons, and its grandsons. The Lord knew that the worldliness of the Canaanites would be a cause of great stumbling
to His people and their children. They needed to be satu-
rated with principles of truth and righteousness if they
were to remain in the revealed faith. The instruction first
given to that generation of Israelites is still bursting with

helpful directives for Christian parents today as they seek to prepare their children to face modern-day paganism.

1. *Notice that the parents were called on to be models of the truth (v. 6).* The words of the law were to be on *their* hearts first. If you and I, as parents, are not modeling the faith as we should be, then we can hardly expect our children to be attracted to it. I am convinced that the faith which some of our children reject is not true Christianity but a distortion of it. They have yet to see the real thing consistently lived out in the home even though their parents claim to be Christians.

It should be noted that the fifth most compelling reason for rejecting the faith, as recorded in the Youth Congress '85 survey, is "poor Christian role models in my home." Parents, our children are watching us. What are they learning from our attitude toward the world and its attractions?

In a book entitled *What They Did Right*, Virginia Hearn records the testimony of thirty-eight Christians from various backgrounds who share the "right" things their parents did which influenced them to adopt the Christian faith. Over and over again, the same message came through: "They lived the Christian life before me; they were models of godly people; they were consistent in their Christian convictions." In other words, these parents had the Law of God upon their own hearts. That is where it must start. We parents must have a heart-religion if we desire our own kids to have one too.

2. *We must teach our children by means of repetition (v. 7).* The words *teach diligently* mean literally, "to say something twice" or "to repeat." They are used to refer to the sharpening of a blade or a tool by repeatedly rubbing the blade against the whetstone. Gradually the word came to mean "to sharpen" and "to pierce" and then "to teach." The idea seems to be that by repeating the teachings of the Law over and over again, parents will drive it into the minds and hearts of their children like a piercing weapon.

Whether or not the author of Hebrews had this word in mind when he referred to God's Word as a piercing sword, I don't know. But there can be little doubt about the thrust of this passage. Our teaching of God's Word must be like the sharpening of a sword through repeated rubbing; it must be done over and over again so that it makes a deep impression on them.

Teaching children so as to lead them into a personal knowledge of the faith cannot be done with a "lick-and-a promise" approach. We must be diligent in our instruction or it will not penetrate. We must use every available means that God provides for us, including the ministries of the church and the Christian schools.

I do not believe this passage suggests that the best or only way to teach our children is through rote learning or memorization of Bible verses and stories and catechism questions. Certainly, the passage does endorse that kind of learning as well as the importance of review, but the primary idea of repetition in this passage, I think, lies in another direction.

3. *We must teach our children by applying God's Word in every situation (vv. 7-9).* What is the Lord telling us to do here? Obviously, He is telling us to teach our children to apply the truths, principles, and commands of His Word to everything we do, morning, noon, and night. He is saying, "Help your children see that My Word applies to every situation in life, that there is nothing in life that is divorced from My will."

In order to help His people better understand this teaching approach, the Lord became very specific. He says in verse 7, "you shall teach them [the commands] diligently to your sons and you shall talk of them when you sit in your house and when you walk by the way and when you lie down and when you rise up." For us today that means if we are sitting around the dinner table and our seven-year-old tells us he is angry with his teacher, we can point him to what God says about forgiveness or patience or respect for those in authority over us. When we are out for a walk at night, we can remind our children that the gorgeous sunset or the glittering heavens are created by the Lord, and then we can teach them how to offer up a prayer of praise to Him in thanksgiving for that specific act of creation. If there is a violent thunderstorm in the middle of the night, we can turn their thoughts to God's power in nature but also to His protective care for His own people.

In other words, this passage tells us that we must integrate biblical truths into every situation of life so that our children will find it quite natural to think of God and His perspective on all things. Jay Adams puts it this way:

> We must teach children that all of life is under God and must become sacred to them. We must teach them that God's Word is all-embracing; there is no neutral ground in all of life; it is to be lived for Him in its entirety. That is why God requires teaching in the milieu of life.[1]

Adams has hit the nail on the head—our children must see that there is no neutral ground in life. Either we look at life from God's perspective or from man's. Christianity must be applied to all of life or it is not true Christianity. Loving and serving God is not something that is to be done only on Sunday. It is to be the motivating factor behind all of the believer's actions. Likewise, the teachings of God's Word are not simply for certain moral situations; they are to be the framework upon which we build our entire philosophy of life—the filter through which we examine every experience.

The commandments of God, says Moses, are to be as a "sign on your hand," and as "frontals on your forehead" (v. 8). They are to be a part of our very being, guiding both our thoughts and our actions. Written "upon the doorposts" of our house (v. 9), they are to govern everything that happens under our roof. When our children grow up with this kind of consistent, God-centered instruction, they will have difficulty ignoring the Christian faith. Granted, the truth must be on *their* hearts too as well as on their parents' hearts, but this "total-saturation" approach to their education set forth in Deuteronomy 6 will establish a solid foundation for our children's ultimate acceptance of and continuance in the Christian faith.

More than half the young people (56 percent) identified "hypocrisy in the church" as one of the potential reasons for forsaking the faith. This charge of hypocrisy, to a large extent, grows out of the teens' failure to see the faith that is professed on Sunday applied to all of life the rest of the week.

I believe one of the most needy areas in this whole subject of raising our kids to abide in the faith is right here: developing in them a consistent Christian view of the world and life. That, of course, is one of the primary aims of the Christian school. But in order to be effective, this kind of training has to start in the home and be supported by the efforts of the parents. God has given parents in particular the stewardship of inculcating on the impressionable minds of our children the truth of God's Word as it relates to all of life.

There is, however, another dimension to this inculcation process that many Christian parents ignore.

INOCULATE AGAINST SPIRITUAL DISEASE

Our children are growing up in a hostile environment. They must ward off many infectious spiritual diseases that could easily impede their development. The number one disease, according to the survey results, is "the attractions of this evil world."

How do we deal with this infection? Some parents say, "We must isolate our kids as much as possible from the things of this world." Some Christian schools have been started for that very reason. As desirable as it may seem, however, the isolationist approach will not work for most families. It will not keep the world from infiltrating our homes and influencing the thinking of our kids.

I would like to propose another approach to dealing with "the negative influence of the world." This approach is actually a natural expansion of the teaching principles we just discussed from Deuteronomy 6. I call it *spiritual inoculation*, defined as the giving of occasional, small, controlled " injections" of an opposing viewpoint accompanied by careful instruction in how to combat that viewpoint. In a Christian context, this means giving small doses of non-Christian thought with a careful critique of such thought from a Christian perspective.

LEARN FROM BIBLICAL EXAMPLES
OF SPIRITUAL INOCULATION

In 1 Kings 18 we have the most powerful display of the spiritual inoculation process in all of Scripture. As a nation, Israel was desperately sick. Through intermingling with the Baal worshipers, all but a remnant of true believers had totally rejected the revealed faith. If Israel were to be saved, the nation would have to be given a megadose of divine medication to halt the progress of unbelief and moral compromise. The people would have to see with their own eyes that there was no comparison between Baal and the Lord. They would have to decide once and for all whom they would serve (1 Kings 18:21).

In allowing the prophets of Baal to cry out to their god first (1 Kings 18:25-29), Elijah permitted the Israelites to observe firsthand the vanity of putting their faith in this false god. But when he followed this "injection" of pagan worship with the "antidote" of the miraculous power of Yahweh (1 Kings 18:20-38), there was an immediate surge of spiritual renewal: the people proclaimed, "The Lord, He is God; the Lord, He is God" (v. 39). This spiritual inoculation shocked their religious systems, at least temporarily, and brought them back to positive spiritual health.

This comparing and contrasting of God's way with the

world's way is crucial to the inoculation process. In Deuteronomy 32, in the song of Moses, the leader of the Israelites seeks to prepare them to deal with the paganism of the Canaanites. He reminds them that the only way Israel met with success in past battles was that the Lord, their Rock, had been on their side (v. 30). Even their enemies recognized this fact: "Indeed their rock is not like our Rock, even our enemies themselves judge this" (v. 31). Moses is probably referring to the Egyptians' response after having their chariots bog down in the mire of the Red Sea: "Let us flee from Israel, for the LORD is fighting for them against the Egyptians" (Ex. 14:25). In his song, Moses is really comparing Israel's God with the gods of the other nations and saying, "Don't even think of following after the gods of the Canaanites. They are no match for our God; even our enemies know that." By contrasting the pagan gods with the true God, Moses is trying to inoculate the Israelites against the paganism of the Canaanites.

The Book of Proverbs contains other illustrations of spiritual inoculation. For example, Proverbs 5:1-23, 6:20-35, and 7:1-27 discuss in great detail the allurements of the adulterous woman, but these passages also warn of the bitter ends of an adulterous relationship and contrast that kind of relationship with obedience to the commands of God.

Not only does Solomon inoculate his son against the evil ways of the sensual woman, but he also warns his son about the ways of the sluggard, the fool, the drunkard, the scoffer, the wicked one, the wealthy one, and sinners in general. In each case, however, he not only describes the character or behavior of the unbelievers, but he also lists the consequences of their actions in contrast to the benefits of following God's way. He first gives the inoculation of the "disease," and then he adds the antidote of righteousness. Indeed, the entire Book of Proverbs can be viewed as one long, continuous spiritual inoculation.

In the New Testament the examples of spiritual inoculation are more subtle than those in the Old Testament. For instance, in Matthew 16:13 Jesus asks His disciples, "Who do people say that the Son of Man is?" In other words, He challenges them to think about the common attitude of the unbelievers with regard to His true identity. When they respond, "Some say John the Baptist; and others Elijah; but still others, Jeremiah, or one of the prophets," Jesus challenges them as to their own convictions: "But who do you say that I am?" (Matt. 16:14-15) He inoculates them by making them focus on the difference between the false views of the day and what they had received as truth from the Father regarding His person.

Several times in the Sermon on the Mount Jesus states: "You have heard that it was said . . . but I say unto you" (Matt. 5:21-44). In each case He is contrasting His own teaching with distorted interpretations of the Old Testament, hopefully inoculating His hearers against the false teaching of the day and thereby strengthening their faith in Him.

AVOID INCUBATION
Most Christian parents tend to do some spiritual inoculating without realizing it. For example, every time we draw attention to some kind of non-Christian behavior or point of view and then give our children the biblical response to it, we are immunizing them against that opposing viewpoint. I am suggesting that Christian parents should *consciously* look for ways to inoculate their children by giving them periodic "shots" of non-Christian thought along with the carefully administered Christian antidote.

Research done by several social psychologists demonstrates both the vulnerability of those who have not been exposed to opposing viewpoints and the ability to resist counterarguments by those who have been previously taught how to handle different points of view. Applying these findings to the Christian faith, educational psychologist Bonnidell Clouse concludes:

Two essential aspects of this process [inoculation] are that children be aware that Christian beliefs may be subject to attack and that they be given the opportunity to develop defenses against the attack. Children raised in an environment in which they have not had opportunity to build up these defenses may succumb when placed in a situation in which "disease" thrives.[3]

Clouse is correct. I can remember a childhood friend whose parents followed a spiritual isolationist approach to parenting rather than a spiritual inoculationist one. He was not allowed to watch any TV or to play with any children in the neighborhood unless they were from our church. He told me years later that he was shocked when he first learned that not everybody believed in Jesus. The sad fact is that as far as I know, my friend does not believe in Jesus either. When he got to college, he quickly threw off his superficial childhood confession and became totally absorbed in a godless lifestyle.

In their early years, our children will tend to identify with our faith and imitate our attitudes, beliefs, and behavior. Because they are constantly exposed to the teachings of Scripture and to life in the Christian community, they will tend to incorporate much of what they observe and learn into their own personality. Their value system will tend to be a Christian value system. Their thinking and conduct will be, basically, a reflection of what they were taught by their parents and the church. Freudian psychologists call this process the "internalization of the superego." Social learning theorists call it, "the development of a conscience." Christian educators refer to it as "personalizing" or "individualizing" the faith of one's parents. It may or may not lead to a genuine conversion experience, but it most certainly plays an important role in the faith development of our children.

As our children approach adolescence, the formative influence of their parents gradually gives way to the influence of their peers. Up to that point, we can probably meet with some success in isolating them from the world. Once they move into the more reflective stage of adolescence, however, they tend to become very curious about the beliefs and behavior of other people, especially their "significant others." If, over the years, we have been incubating our children instead of inoculating them, they may have a very difficult time with these new views and lifestyles. In many cases they may be totally overwhelmed by them and end up jettisoning the Christian faith in the process. But if we have made a practice of carefully exposing our children to the contaminating ways of the world and contrasting these ways with the Christian way, they are less likely to be overwhelmed by the influx of new ideas and lifestyles.

KNOW WHEN AND HOW TO INOCULATE
But how does this process of spiritual inoculation occur? Let me give you just one example. I'm sure you would agree that the number one source for the communication of non-Christian value systems is the television.[4] While your children are young, you should carefully monitor their use of the TV. But as they get older, they will have to be given more freedom in this matter. You will have to trust them as to how much time they spend watching the TV and what they are viewing. It is important, therefore, to get in the habit of discussing with them, in their pre-adolescent years, the various moral and religious issues that are presented on the screen.

In particular, we should ask questions about the specific actions of people and the attitudes or beliefs behind their words and actions. For instance, assume you are watching the evening news with your nine-year-old, and you watch a report about a man beating up his wife and children. The temptation will be either to ignore the incident or simply to say, "Isn't that terrible!" and hope that your daughter understands why a father would do such a terrible thing. But to make either response is to ignore a natural opportunity to do some spiritual inoculating. Instead, you could ask your child questions such as: "Why did the man act that way? Who was he most concerned about? What would Jesus say to a man like that? What should the man have done?" By discussing this news report you are teaching values right in the milieu of life; you are fulfilling Deuteronomy 6 by teaching your children how to apply God's law to a situation that has arisen as you are sitting in your own home.

Sunday School teachers and Christian school teachers also have a responsibility to assist parents in this inoculation process. I've always appreciated the teachers in the Christian school my three children attended for making the effort to inoculate their students in the different areas of knowledge. In the sciences, the humanities, the arts, or even on the basketball court, these teachers did not ignore the non-Christian viewpoint or leave it uncritiqued. Unfortunately, some Christian schools are not attempting to inoculate our children from the world. Instead, they are doing the exact opposite—they are trying to isolate them from the world. But when parents, teachers, and administrators understand the value of the principle of spiritual inoculation as it applies to all of life, the Christian school can be one of the greatest sources of regular spiritual "injections" as our children are "walking in the way."

One thing is clear, if faith rejection occurs, the blame cannot be laid at the door of the school. The main problem is in the home. A child's enticement to the world begins within his own family context. I suspect that some parents have given their children unnecessary exposure to the philosophy and behavior of the world. Giving them a Playboy magazine to teach them about the world's view of sex will not inoculate them; it may do the very opposite, namely, create an unhealthy interest in sex. Remember, inoculations must be *controlled*. We do not want to give an overdose of worldly thought but rather periodic, small, controlled amounts. If we can't control the dosage, we shouldn't give it.

Some parents may try to expose their children to non-Christian thinking, but they fail to consistently administer the Christian antidote to such ideas. Or, in discussing a non-Christian's position on something, they may fail to communicate a fair representation of that position. For example, it is possible to give the impression that all those who favor abortion are wicked people who hate unborn babies. But if that is what we teach our children, we are building a straw man that will be quickly blown down by the arguments of the pro-choice activists. We must present non-Christian thought as honestly and as clearly as possible. If we don't, our children may later think we were trying to deceive them with half-truths, and they may end up resenting us for it.

Spiritual inoculation is not meant to be an excuse for Christians to flirt with the world. The warnings of Scripture still stand: "Abstain from every form of evil" (1 Thes. 5:22); "Flee from youthful lusts" (2 Tim. 2:22); "Do not be conformed to this world" (Rom. 12:2). Christian parents ought to be modeling this true, biblical isolationism. But there is definitely room in the Christian home for both wise, protective isolation and ongoing inoculation.

Sadly, some parents have compromised so much with the way the world thinks and acts that they themselves have become squeezed into its mold. And so they have opened themselves up to the charge of hypocrisy and have probably lost the respect and the ear of their children. They can't say "do as I do" when they know they are not living godly lives themselves; nor can they effectively keep their children from developing a similar worldly mindset.

There can be no doubt that God holds Christian parents responsible for preparing their children to enter and live in "the land of the pagans." His basic preparation methods are the same today as they were when Moses challenged the parents of his generation. By our lives and lips we must inculcate in them the principles of His Word, and we must spiritually inoculate them against the evils of this world.

For Review, Discussion, and Action:

1. What are the four primary reasons for rejecting the faith as identified in the Youth Congress '85 questionnaire? What does this suggest about the kind of pressures placed on our children today?

2. Based on Deuteronomy 6:4-9, what are the three specific ways we are to inculcate the truth in our children? Which of the three ways are you incorporating into the training of your children? Which ones need improving?

3. List several specific ways you have been, or could be, applying the truths of God's Word to your daily experiences with your children as you "walk by the way."

4. Define *spiritual inoculation.*

5. Compare the advantages and disadvantages of isolating our children from the world with inoculating them against the world.

6. Think back to your own childhood. Did your parents, if Christians, try to inoculate you against the world or isolate you from it? How did you react to their efforts? What would you do the same as they did? What would you do differently?

7. Discuss various ways spiritual inoculation can occur in the home, in the Christian school, and in the church.

8. After studying this chapter, what specific actions do you believe you should take as a parent? What obstacles do you foresee and how could you overcome them?

For Further Study:

Coleman, William L. *Making TV Work for Your Family.*
Minneapolis: Bethany House Publishers, 1983. This is a
very enjoyable and helpful little book on the subject of a
Christian approach to watching TV. It is designed for
families to read together as a means of developing a
constructive use of their television sets.

CHAPTER FOUR

KEEP THEM FROM THE EVIL ONE

Faith-formation Principle: *To help our children come to an enduring faith in Christ, we must seek to keep them from the evil one by teaching them what it means to live* **in** *the world without being* **of** *the world.*

Biblical Texts: John 17:15-16; 1 John 2:15-17

My wife was only fifteen at the time. She had been taught never to enter a movie house because movies were the epitome of worldliness. But there she was with her girlfriend in a theater in downtown Ottawa, watching her first movie. She recalls that it was about the life of a prostitute. Beyond that, all she can remember is that before the movie was half over she and her girlfriend were so afraid that the Lord would come back and find them in a theater that they got up and left.

The cause of their guilt was not so much the film itself but the fact that their consciences had been trained to accuse them for watching any movie in a theater. (The content of the film by today's standards was quite tame.) Many of you reading these words know exactly what I'm talking about. You, like me, were taught by parents and

pastors that playing cards, dancing, attending movie the-
aters, and numerous other activities were taboo for Christians. Such activities, we were told, were condemned by
the Bible as worldly. Whenever we asked where the Bible
condemned these things, we were usually quoted 1 Thessa-
lonians 5:22: "Avoid every appearance [form] of evil" (KJV).
But we were never given any principles or guidelines to
help us understand what evil is and what evil is not; we
were just given a list of activities generally considered to
be evil by the evangelical church in the mid-1950s.

Today, in the late-1980s, I'm sure that such a list still
exists in many churches, creating just as much confusion,
anger, and rebellion among children of Christian parents as
it did when I was a teenager. Unfortunately, a list of do's
and don'ts will never help our young people deal with the
lure of the world's attractions. We can never protect adolescents from the struggle of deciding for themselves how
they are to face worldly temptations. We should never try
to protect them from such a struggle; it is a necessary
means of developing character and responsibility in their
lives. The list-of-evils approach greatly retards this maturing process. It causes our children unnecessary guilt and
frustration, and it inhibits their freedom and ability to become Christian decision-makers.

We have already observed in the previous chapter that
the number one potential cause of faith rejection, as indicated from the Youth Congress '85 survey, is "the attractions of the world." In Deuteronomy 6 we saw that our
children must look at all of life through the spectacles of
God's Word and that part of this broad view involves spiritually inoculating them against the godless thinking and
actions of the unbelievers around them. We must gradually
acquaint them with the philosophy and lifestyle of the
world but at the same time clearly state the accompanying
Christian "antidote." To try to isolate our children from the
world by hedging them in with an arbitrary list of do's and
don'ts is deceitful, dangerous, and just plain dumb.

But why do our young people find the attractions of the world so appealing? And what is it about the biblical concept of the world that causes us as Christians to speak negatively about worldly attractions and worldliness? Did not God create this world and everything in it and then pronounce the finished product good? Did not the Apostle Paul tell young Timothy that "everything created by God is good, and nothing is to be rejected, if it is received with gratitude"? (1 Tim. 4:4) If this is true, then why does the Christian conscience struggle over much of what this "good" world offers?

The answer to these questions is found when we come to grips with a basic truth taught by Jesus in John 17. Jesus is aware that He will soon be departing from this world and leaving His disciples to struggle on their own. Knowing this, He prays for His followers and for those who would come to faith through their ministry: "I do not ask Thee to take them out of the world, but to keep them from the evil one. They are not of the world, even as I am not of the world" (John 17:15-16). Worldliness is a struggle for believers because they are "in" this world but not "of" it.

KNOW THAT BELIEVERS ARE NOT OF THE WORLD

Jesus recognizes that He and His followers are not of the world. It's easy to understand how He can say, "I am not of the world" because He came from His Father in heaven. But in what sense are His followers not of this world? It would appear that, in part at least, Jesus is thinking of the new spiritual natures we possess as those who have born "from above" (John 3:3). In other words, in terms of the origin of our reborn natures, we are not of this world. But neither are we of this world in terms of our ultimate allegiance. Paul says in Philippians 3:20 that our citizenship is in heaven. It is to this heavenly allegiance that Jesus is referring when He says we are not of this world.

The very word *world* (cosmos) carries the idea of an allegiance to Satan. As used by the Apostle John, the word *world* can have several different meanings.[1] Here in John 17 the context indicates that Jesus is thinking about the world as it exists in a state of rebellion against its Maker. Our Lord's references to "evil" or "the evil one" suggest that, in His mind, Satan and the evil enticements of the world are closely connected. Jesus refers to Satan elsewhere as the "ruler of this world" (John 12:31; 14:30; 16:11). In this capacity, Satan has been permitted certain restricted freedoms. For example, the whole world lies under his power, but he cannot touch the one who has been born of God (1 John 5:18-19).

So believers are "not of this world" because they have been set free from the power of the "god of this age." They have been given a new, "heavenly" nature, a new allegiance to the kingdom of God, and a new freedom from Satan's touch. They have even been given the new responsibility and ability to seek first the kingdom of God and His righteousness instead of longing for all the things of the world (Matt. 6:33).

But what does this have to do with helping our children face the attractions of the world? To a large extent the answer lies in how well we, as their parents, demonstrate that we are not of this world. What do our children see in our attitudes and actions toward the world? If all we do is religiously follow a list of do's and don'ts and ignore what it really means to be "not of this world," we will fail to give our children the tools they need to learn how to make their own wise choices about the world's attractions.

We must teach them, by both precept and example, that worldliness is not so much a question of what they do or don't do as it is a matter of the allegiances and affections of their hearts. It's a question of what they are seeking after *first*. John White, in his excellent book *Flirting with the World*, defines worldliness as, "the spirit of the age" and "legitimate desires pursued or exalted to the point of idolatry."[2] Worldliness involves taking on the character of the world in its state of rebellion against God. It has to do with seeking after the things of this world as ends in themselves instead of as blessings from God for our good and His glory.

Our children need to know that God made this world as a place to be viewed as good, to be received with thanksgiving (1 Tim. 4:4), and to be a blessing to mankind (Gen. 1:29-31). But they also must be told that, in its fallen condition, it has become a world in rebellion against its Creator. Sinful men have taken the things of this world and used them for their own selfish and lustful ends instead of as a means of praising God (Rom. 1:21-25). Christians, however, are to be different in their attitude toward the world. The problem is many of us are not that much different. Oh, we may have drawn up a list of certain activities from which we will outwardly abstain but, at the same time, we are secretly lusting after the very things the world lusts after and values most. We are like the respected church leader who told me proudly that he would never darken the door of a movie theater for that was the devil's house, but this man freely admitted to watching R-rated movies in the privacy of his home. This is the height of hypocrisy and reveals a total lack of understanding of the real nature of worldliness. Unfortunately, many Christian parents have conveyed just such an attitude to their children, thereby giving them even further reason to reject the faith.

In recent years I have observed an alarming number of Christians grasping for more of this world's treasures (money, security, power, style, entertainment, possessions, etc.). The Apostle Paul describes this as allowing the world to conform us to its image or to squeeze us into its mold (Rom. 12:1-2). Even as they faithfully adhere to their sacred list of taboos, many Christians are also "laying up treasures on earth." Jesus says this cannot be done. We can't serve two masters (Matt. 6:24).

God's Word calls us to be different. We are to be light and salt to a dark, decaying world. But that difference should not consist primarily in our actions; it should consist in the attitudes, motives, and affections of our hearts. When those inner impulses are tuned to seek first the kingdom of God and His righteousness, we will not likely be led into worldly pursuits. But when our inner longings are fueled by pride, lust, covetousness, or selfishness, we will very likely end up doing what can properly be called worldly activities.

UNDERSTAND SATAN'S APPROACH

Jesus' prayer for us is that we be kept from evil, or better, from the evil one. He desires to leave us in this world, but He does not want us to be in any way influenced by its evil influences or master. Christian parents should have the same concern for their own children. Many of us struggle to know how best to keep our children from the attractions of the world that often lead to evil, but we give little thought to how best keep them from the "evil one" under whose power the whole world lies (1 John 5:19).

Ultimately, of course, only Jesus Christ can deliver our sons and daughters from the binding power of Satan. In leading them to faith in Christ, we lead them to true liberty over sin's curse, sin's dominating power, and sin's chief advocate—the devil. As John says of the one who has been born of God, "the evil one does not touch him" (1 John 5:18). "Not touch," it should be noted, does not mean "not tempt" or "not attack" or "not oppress." Obviously, even though Satan's hold over believers was broken at the Cross (Heb. 2:14-15), he is very active in opposing their growth in godliness (1 Peter 5:8) and their success in ministering the Gospel (2 Tim. 4:17). For that very reason we are called upon to resist him with all our might (Eph. 6:10-20).

If the evil one is still able to attack believers, how much more is he able to influence unbelievers, including children raised in Christian homes? The fact that our children are within the sphere of Gospel influence (1 Cor. 7:14) does not mean they are insulated against the fiery darts of the enemy; perhaps it even makes them his special targets. One thing is certain—Satan's basic approach never changes. He will always seek to hold unbelievers in his kingdom by the enticements of this present evil world. And based on the results of our questionnaire, he is still being highly successful with this standard tactic.

In 1 John 2:15-17 the apostle warns:

> Do not love the world, nor the things in the world. If anyone loves the world, the love of the Father is not in him. For all that is in the world, the lust of the flesh and the lust of the eyes and the boastful pride of life, is not from the Father, but is from the world. And the world is passing away, and also its lusts; but the one who does the will of God abides forever.

John was familiar with Satan's *modus operandi.* We should be also, as Christian parents. He uses the things of this world to appeal to our flesh, our eyes, and our pride. He has followed this approach right from the very beginning when he tempted Adam and Eve. In Genesis 3:6 we read, "When the woman saw that the tree was good for food [the lust of the flesh], and that it was a delight to the eyes [the lust of the eyes], and that the tree was desirable to make one wise [the pride of life], she took from its fruit and ate. . . ." Thousands of years later Satan appealed to Jesus in the wilderness with basically the same three temptations (Matt. 4:3-10). And we can be sure that his approach to us and our children is little different today.

From the very beginning, the evil one has used physical objects to tempt men to disobey God. With the benefits of modern technology and the resultant abundance of material possessions, he has at his disposal a host of temporal things to entice our children away from the faith. Through the means of TV advertising alone he is able to attack our children in all three of the areas in which he tempted Adam and Eve and our Lord: "For only $85.00 you can have that beautiful, sleek ten speed bike (lust of the eyes) which you have always wanted for your own (lust of the flesh) and become the most envied kid in your neighborhood (pride of life)."

RESIST THE EVIL ONE

But how can we, as those who are in the world but not of the world, best keep ourselves and our children from the evil one? What should we be doing in order to resist his appeals to the lust of the flesh, the lust of the eyes, and the pride of life?

The Apostle Paul's arsenal of spiritual weapons in Ephesians 6 is given to help us fight against the powers of darkness as they are at work in the world. The guidelines to be discussed in the rest of this chapter should be viewed as supplementary to that spiritual armor. These guidelines are not meant to provide an exhaustive list of guaranteed steps to victory over the world. No such list exists.

Furthermore, it is to be understood that none of these suggestions will make much impact on our children unless, and until, they are characteristic of our own lives. If we want our children to develop a biblically balanced view of the world and the strength to live godly lives in it, we must lead the way.

1. *In addition to spiritually inoculating our children, as we discussed in chapter 3, we must emphasize God's abiding laws.* We know that certain activities are not acceptable to God. I am thinking about the moral laws of God as revealed in the Ten Commandments. Idolatry, murder, lying, covetousness, disobedience to parents, etc., will always be wrong simply because they are contrary to the very character and will of God. We should not hesitate to teach our children to obey God's moral laws without question.

With the teaching of Jesus, morality even became a question of the thoughts and desires of one's heart (Matt. 5:21-28). Although unregenerate children are morally incapable of consistently obeying the revealed laws of God (at least from the heart), we must faithfully instruct them to do so. The commandments of God are His standards for all mankind, and the fact that our children (or anyone else) cannot measure up to them does not lessen man's accountability before God to keep them.

That is precisely why our children need to hear the Gospel message. They need to know that "all have sinned and fall short of the glory of God" (Rom. 3:23) and that "the wages of sin is death, but the free gift of God is eternal life in Christ Jesus our Lord" (Rom. 6:23). They need to know that Christ kept the Law perfectly for them and that He died to endure its curse. Parents should remember that the inability of their children to keep God's laws could be the very thing that drives them to Christ for salvation. Such was the case with the Apostle Paul when he realized the Law condemned his covetous spirit (Rom. 7:7-12). We must demand our children's obedience to the moral laws of God even as we encourage them to come to faith in Christ.

2. *We must avoid a "Christian laws" mentality.* The problem most of us have is resisting the temptation to add to the revealed moral laws of God. We have already discussed the problems associated with having a list of do's and don'ts. That is basically what the Pharisees did, much to Jesus' displeasure. In Matthew 23:24 He accuses them of being "blind guides, who strain out a gnat and swallow a camel." In other words, they majored on minors (tithing mint, dill, and cumin) while ignoring the more important things (justice, mercy, and faithfulness). Modern-day Pharisees are more likely to strain out the gnats of theater attendance, alcoholic beverages, stylish dress, and season tickets to the symphony. Then they swallow the camels of a grumbling, discontented spirit, a dishonest deal at work, and a gossiping tongue on the phone. They major on the minors of the level of hemlines, necklines, and hairlines while minoring on the majors of compassion, friendship, and forgiveness. Saddest of all, they regard their acts of

spirituality as true righteousness. Jesus is disgusted with such prideful, hypocritical actions. Our children will be too.

3. *We must establish biblical guidelines for the gray areas.* Most of the things we have to deal with regarding the question of worldliness fall into the category of the adiaphora or "things indifferent." That means the Scriptures do not give clear approval or disapproval of them; they give only general principles to help believers determine how to respond. We often speak of these kinds of activities as Christian liberty issues, which means that every Christian is free to make up his or her own mind about how to behave in regard to these matters. In other words, two believers may disagree about activities or forms of entertainment without either of them being morally wrong, that is, as long as they are fulfilling the guidelines set forth in Scripture. In Paul's day "things indifferent" included such things as being a vegetarian or being a meat-eater, eating meat offered to idols or not eating it, observing certain feast days or not observing them (Rom. 14:1-15:3; 1 Cor. 8:1-13; 10:23-33).

In our day the gray areas are different. In fact, they are different from one culture to another. All we can do at this point is set forth some of the basic principles that God's Word gives us and trust they will guide us and our children to make the appropriate decisions. Following are a few questions that we should ask ourselves as we seek to determine the acceptability or unacceptability of a specific action:

● Am I fully convinced in my own mind that this activity is right for me, or does my conscience condemn me? (Rom. 14:5)

● Can I do it in faith? (Rom. 14:22-23)

● Am I truly thankful for the proposed activity or item to be received? (Rom. 14:6; 1 Cor. 10:30)

● Am I acting in submission to Christ as Lord? (Rom. 14:6-9)

● Am I willing to be judged for my actions? (Rom. 14:10-12)

● Will my action put an obstacle or a stumbling block in a brother's way? (Rom. 14:13-15, 21; 1 Cor. 8:9-13)

● Will I offend a brother's conscience? (Rom. 14:20; 1 Cor. 10:28-29)

● Will I be making peace and edifying others? (Rom. 14:19)

● Do I have my neighbor's good in mind? (Rom. 15:2; 1 Cor. 10:24)

● Will this activity profit and edify me? (1 Cor. 10:23)

● Does it bring glory to God? (1 Cor. 10:31)

● Does it hinder or help men come to Christ? (1 Cor. 10:33)

Obviously, it is much easier for us to ignore these guidelines either by setting up our own preferred taboo list or by just doing as we please with no concern for how the exercise of our liberty affects the Lord, our brothers, or ourselves. Unfortunately, most Christians take one of these two routes rather than the harder one of applying the above principles to their behavior. Just like the Galatian believers of Paul's day, we move toward either a legalistic solution or a licentious one. In either case, our children fail to learn how to live as those who are in the world but not of it.

It's time Christians began to take seriously the biblical guidelines for acceptable behavior in these gray areas. We must allow these guidelines to control our own conduct, and we must teach them to our children also. Perhaps we tend to ignore these principles because what they are really calling us to do is to put others ahead of ourselves. They are calling on us to be willing to give up our rights and freedoms in Christ out of love for the brethren. In short, they are demanding that we treat others just as Christ treated us (Rom. 15:3).

4. *We must stress the attitude of the heart.* The Apostle Paul tells us that "the kingdom of God is not eating and drinking, but righteousness and peace and joy in the Holy Spirit" (Rom. 14:17; see also Matt. 23:23). In God's eyes the attitude and condition of the heart are more important than our external actions. That means we must always encourage our children to check their motives and their goals in whatever they do. Often activities become worldly, not because they are inherently evil but because we do them with selfish attitudes or sinful motives. We lust after them or, as John White puts it, we allow legitimate desires to be pursued or exalted to the point of idolatry.[3]

This means that we can be doing totally acceptable things but with worldly motives. For example, I recently joined a fitness center in an attempt to alleviate headaches caused in part by weak back and neck muscles. Some people may view my three hours a week in a coed "sweat house" as a worldly activity; however, because my motives are honoring to the Lord, and as far as I can discern, the activities I engage in meet the tests of the above guidelines, I feel free to continue. If I discover that my motives for going to the gym shift from maintaining good health to building a beautiful body that all will admire or to providing an excuse for gazing on members of the opposite sex, then I will be guilty of worldliness, and I will feel compelled to drop my membership. God looks on our hearts. Man looks on our outward appearance. We must be concerned about both.

Jesus calls on us to be light and salt in a dark and decaying world. That means we will be different from the unbe-lievers around us. At times the difference will be so great that the world will hate us (Matt. 5:11-16). They will hate us, though, not because we follow some strict list of do's and don'ts, but because we are obviously "not of this world." We have a different nature than they do, a different allegiance, and a different agenda.

We can best help our children escape the power of the evil one and the attractions of the world by teaching them how to view God's world biblically. We must never forget, however, that we are in a battle for the souls of our chil-dren and that our primary struggle is "not against flesh and blood, but against . . . the forces of darkness, against the spiritual forces of wickedness in the heavenly places" (Eph. 6:12). All of our efforts, therefore, must be bathed with fervent prayer for their salvation and spiritual growth. Only then can we have great confidence in His faithfulness to give both us and our children victory over the evil one and his worldly temptations. As John puts it in 1 John 5:3-5:

> For this is the love of God, that we keep His com-mandments; and His commandments are not bur-densome. For whatever is born of God overcomes the world; and this is the victory that has overcome the world—our faith. And who is the one who over-comes the world, but he who believes that Jesus is the Son of God?

For Review, Discussion, and Action:

1. Define *worldliness* so as to reflect the common evan-gelical taboos of today. Now write a definition based on the biblical information given in this chapter. What are the basic differences?

2. Identify three points Jesus likely has in mind when He says we are not of this world.

3. Read Matthew 23:24 and give examples of modern-day Pharisaism in the church.

4. Based on 1 John 2:15-17, give examples of how the lust of the flesh, the lust of the eyes, and the pride of life can be used by Satan to tempt our children to worldliness.

5. List five things parents must do to keep their children from the evil one. Which one would be the most difficult for you? Why?

6. Identify any activities in your own life that are worldly and determine what God would have you do about them.

7. After reviewing the twelve guidelines regarding "things indifferent" (pp. 63-64), formulate a plan for helping your children decide whether or not an activity is worldly.

For Further Study:

Field, David. *Free to Do Right*. Downers Grove: InterVarsity Press, 1973. Field gives us helpful directives in how to make moral decisions by keeping our focus on the revealed character and law of God.

White, John. *Flirting with the World*. Wheaton: Harold Shaw Publishers, 1982. This is a thought-provoking challenge to the evangelical church at large regarding its present understanding of worldliness. White suggests the biblical way out of the dilemma we have made for ourselves by our straining of gnats and swallowing of camels.

CHAPTER FIVE

AIM FOR THE HEART

Faith-formation Principle: To help our children come to an enduring faith in Christ, we must bring the claims of the Gospel to bear on their outward behavior, but especially on their hearts.

Biblical Texts: Matthew 15:1-9; Proverbs 4:23; 21:2
Barbara had grown up as a preacher's kid. For most of her teenage life she had conformed, outwardly, to the expected evangelical lingo and lifestyle. Inwardly, however, she was stubbornly resisting the claims of the Gospel. She was intellectually convinced that Christianity was true but, in her heart, she wanted nothing to do with it. She told me, "I was phony. My parents never knew the true me because I worked hard at concealing who I really was. They were naive parents."[1]

I wonder how many other concerned, Christian parents are similarly naive about what their children are *really* thinking about the faith. Barbara's testimony is not unique. All of us know parents (perhaps we are such ourselves) who thought their children were true believers but were shocked to discover a spirit of rebellion that led them away from the church and into the world. Some, like Barbara, came back. Others did not.

How can we avoid being so naive about the spiritual condition of our children? And how can we help our children avoid becoming phonies of the faith who feel they must put on the Christian veneer in order to be loved and accepted by parents and church? These are important questions which demand far more attention than I can give in just one chapter; however, I can suggest what I believe is one thing we *must* do as parents. If we want to lead our children to be open about their relationship with God and if we want them to come to an enduring faith in Christ, we must aim for their hearts.

AVOID RAISING LITTLE HYPOCRITES
In the previous chapter we observed that hypocrisy in adults is one of the leading causes of faith rejection among children raised in Christian homes. We must realize, however, that our children themselves can develop a very convincing pharisaical spirit. They can be living and saying one thing outwardly while believing the exact opposite inwardly. As harsh as it may sound, they can be growing up as little hypocrites.

But what precisely is a hypocrite? In Matthew 15 the scribes and Pharisees came to Jesus complaining that His disciples had broken the tradition of the elders by eating with unwashed hands (vv. 1-2). Jesus turns the tables by pointing to the Pharisees' more serious practice of breaking the Law of God in order to keep their own man-made traditions (vv. 3-6). But the most significant part of this exchange is Jesus' interpretation of the Pharisees' behavior. After calling them "hypocrites," He quotes from Isaiah 29:13 and applies the prophet's rebuke of Israel to the Pharisees themselves:

This people honors Me with their lips, but their heart is far away from Me. But in vain do they worship Me, teaching as doctrines the precepts of men (Matt. 15:8-9).

Jesus defines the hypocrisy of the Pharisees (and their forefathers) as the act of saying something with their lips that they do not believe in their hearts.

The heart attitude is central to true faith and true worship. When our children grow up with the impression that what pleases us the most is what they *say* (using the right evangelical vocabulary, singing the hymns in church, talking politely, etc.) and how they *act* (going to church without complaint, participating in family devotions, giving outward obedience, etc.), they can very easily begin doing these things for the wrong reasons. Children generally want to please their parents. But the problem is that "the heart is more deceitful than all else and is desperately sick" (Jer. 17:9). What may begin as an honest desire to make Mom and Dad happy can very quickly degenerate into a ploy to "keep them off my case." An unregenerate heart, even in those who are being raised within the sphere of Gospel influence, will ultimately reveal its true nature. In other words, unless God gives them new hearts, our children may learn to play the role of a Christian until ultimately they will shed their cloak of hypocrisy and reveal their true, rebellious natures.

CONCENTRATE ON THE HEART

But why are we expressing so much concern over the hearts of our children? Are not their outward actions and their ultimate choices in life more important than what they think in their hearts? No! Not if we accept the teaching of Scripture. Solomon, for example, was eager to convey to his son the centrality of the heart. Consider the following two verses:

Watch over your heart with all diligence, for from it flow the springs of life (Prov. 4:23).

Every man's way is right in his own eyes, but the
LORD weighs the hearts (Prov. 21:2).

In these two verses Solomon gives us the two most important reasons in all of Scripture for concentrating our efforts
on the hearts of our children. What he is telling his sons,
and what we must communicate to our children, is that
they must constantly guard their heart attitudes and motives because their hearts are the source of life and their
hearts will be judged by the Lord. Let's look briefly at each
of these two reasons.

1. *Our hearts are the source of life* (Prov. 4:23).The ultimate source of life, of course, is the Creator of all things—
the one, true God of the Bible. He created physical life and
spiritual life. But just as we speak of human life being in
the blood or flowing from the human heart, so also we can
speak of spiritual life as issuing or springing from the
heart. In the Bible, the heart is viewed as the fulcrum of
feeling and faith as well as the source of our words and
actions. It is the control center for our mind, emotion, and
will.

Both good and evil can spring forth from this fountain-
head of life; it all depends on the nature of the heart. Jesus
told the Pharisees of His day that "the mouth speaks out of
that which fills the heart" (Matt. 12:34) and that "out of the
heart come evil thoughts, murders, adulteries, fornications,
thefts, false witness, slanders" (Matt. 15:19). In other
words, the heart is the source of one's words and one's
actions.

When our children speak or act in an ungodly way, we
must realize that their words and actions are the fruit of
what they are in the very core of their being. And we must
somehow communicate this important truth to them. They
need to be challenged as to the real motives behind the
sinful things they say and do; they need to understand that
Jesus says their behavior is "defiled" (Matt. 15:18-20) and
like "bad fruit" because of the "evil treasure" of their

hearts (Matt. 12:33-35). Many times our small children *feel* that their behavior is wrong, but they don't know why. Their conscience is doing its work (Rom. 2:14-15), but they don't *understand* why they are acting the way they are.[2] Granted, our smallest children are not able to engage in logical or self-reflective thinking. But even when they are too young to think conceptually, we should begin to help them develop the habit of looking inward. We should urge them to ask the question, *why?*—"Why did I say such a mean thing?" or "Why did I hit my brother in anger?" Simply telling them, "Mommy and Daddy and Jesus do not like that kind of behavior. Stop doing it," will not help them. We need to help them focus on the inner source of the problem and look upward to the real solution. If we don't, they may develop into little hypocrites and then big, pharisaical hypocrites.

2. *A second reason Solomon gives for focusing on the heart is that our hearts will be judged by the Lord.* In Proverbs 21:2 he says "Every man's (child's) way is right in his own eyes, but the LORD weighs the hearts." This reminds us of the Lord's comment to Samuel regarding his choosing of a king for Israel from the sons of Jesse. He said, "God sees not as man sees, for man looks on the outward appearance, but the LORD looks at the heart" (1 Sam. 16:7).

It is basic to the nature of man, including children who are being raised within the sphere of Gospel influence, to be more interested in the external appearance or the visible behavior of man than in the attitude of the heart. This does not in any way mean that we are to ignore the significance of man's outward conduct; however, the whole point of our Lord's challenge of the Pharisees' hypocritical spirit is that their outward behavior was not a true expression of their inner motivation. They could not hide their *real* desires from the all-seeing eyes of God, and God could not ignore those inner desires in His judgment of them (Matt. 12:34-37).

It is incumbent upon parents, then, to lovingly remind their children that God sees and understands all (Ps. 139:1-2). Not only does He know what is in their hearts, but He also holds them responsible for their heart attitudes; therefore, the important question for them to ask themselves is not, "Was what I said or did right in *my* eyes?" but rather, "Was what I said or did right in *God's* eyes?"

Some parents may think this emphasis on God judging the motives of the heart will produce in their children a negative concept of God as well as a poor self-image. The matter of self-esteem or self-image is another whole issue which we cannot consider here.[3] But we need not fear that our children will develop a negative attitude toward God when we stress His interest in their heart-attitudes if we also give them the other side of the picture. God does look at the attitudes of the heart and make His judgments accordingly. On the other hand, He is a God who does not reward us according to our iniquities (Ps. 103:10) but has provided a way of escape in His Son, Jesus Christ. That is why, whenever we confront our children about their heart attitudes and about God's examining of their hearts, we should also remind them of the good news of the Gospel. We should never inflict the wounds without giving the healing balm as well. When we give the whole picture, in language that can be understood by our children at their particular stage of growth, we do not have to fear that they will develop a distorted idea of God and His dealings with them.

So far, we have noted that we aim for our children's hearts because (1) their hearts are the source of life and (2) their hearts will be judged by the Lord. There is one final reason why we must focus our attention upon the hearts of our children.

3. *It is with their hearts that our children must believe in Christ for salvation.* In Romans 10:9-10 the Apostle Paul writes, "If you confess with your mouth Jesus as Lord, and believe in your *heart* that God raised Him from the dead,

you shall be saved; for with the *heart* man believes, resulting in righteousness, and with the mouth he confesses,
resulting in salvation"(emphasis added). Confessing with
the mouth—simply saying "I'm a Christian"—is not sufficient for salvation; one must trust from the heart in the
risen Saviour. It is not even enough for our children to
believe in their heads that Jesus is the only way; the de-
mons possess that kind of faith and shudder (James 2:19).
Heart faith—faith that affects the mind, emotions, and
will—is the only kind of faith that leads to salvation and
that endures to the very end.

LEARN HOW TO AIM FOR THE HEART

It is much easier to identify biblical reasons for aiming at
the hearts of our children than it is to set forth methods
that are most likely to penetrate their hearts with the life-
changing power of the Gospel. As the Puritan Flavel wrote,
"The greatest difficulty in conversion is to win the heart to
God, and after conversion to keep it with Him."[4] This is so,
not only because Satan will do everything in his power to
hold on to the hearts of our children, but also because
changing their hearts is ultimately the sovereign work of
the Holy Spirit. Both in its inception (John 3:3-8) and in its
continuance (Jude 24), spiritual life is God's free and gracious gift that can be appropriated by our children only by
simple faith (Eph. 2:8-9).

Even though salvation is the work of God alone, He does
involve man. Our efforts become the very instruments
through which He accomplishes His predetermined plan
(see Jude 21, 24; Phil. 2:12-13). It is essential, therefore, that
we give some thought to the question of how God would
have us bring the Gospel to bear on the hearts of our
children so that they would respond in faith. Hopefully, the
following suggestions will be a help in that direction.

1. *We must never hesitate to apply the Word of God to
the conversation and behavior of our children.* This sug-
gestion is in keeping with our earlier discussion of Deuter-

onomy 6:4-7 where Moses instructed the people of Israel to apply God's commands to their own hearts first, and then to the daily, life experiences of their children. In Hebrews 4:12 the author declares that "the word of God is living and active and sharper than any two-edged sword, and piercing as far as the division of soul and spirit, of both joints and marrow, and able to judge the thoughts and intentions of the heart." God's Word is His sword for piercing the hearts of our children. It alone will not return void (Isa. 55:11).

There are certain occasions in the lives of most children when their hearts may be especially open to the piercing effect of carefully selected passages of Scripture. For instance, consider the following situations and accompanying verses:

● Lying (Prov. 19:9; Acts 5:1-6; Rev. 21:8).

● Stealing (Ex. 20:15; Josh. 7:19-26; Eph. 4:28).

● Disobeying parents (Ex. 20:12; Deut. 21:18-21; Eph. 6:1-3).

● Jealousy, envy (Gen. 37:4; Prov. 23:17; James 3:13-18).

● Abuse of bodies through gluttony, drugs, alcohol, or sex (1 Cor. 6:9-20; Gal. 5:19-21)

● Pain caused by unkind words or actions of other children (Matt. 5:10-12; Rom. 12:17-21).

● Childhood fears (1 Sam. 12:22; Ps. 91; Matt. 10:28; 1 John 4:18).

On one occasion, my youngest daughter, Lynn, came home in tears because she had been teased about being a preacher's kid who wore clothes from K-Mart. We talked about how God looks not on the outward appearance but on the heart (1 Sam. 16:7) and about what motivated the other children to say the mean things they had said (Matt. 12:35-37; 15:18-20). But it was when I shared from 1 Peter 2:19-23 about Jesus being reviled and treated unjustly yet not reviling in return, that Lynn seemed to be most comforted. God's Word ministered to her specific need in a way that neither Mom nor Dad could.

If we want our children's hearts to be motivated to believe in the Gospel and to grow strong in the faith, we must be quick to confront them with the powerful and living Word of God, especially when they are struggling with situations like those listed above. It is only in the Scriptures that they will find life for their souls (John 5:39-40; 6:68).

2. *We must seek to touch the mind, emotions, and will of our children with the Word of God.* If the heart is the center of our children's thoughts, feelings, and actions, it only stands to reason that we should appeal to all three dimensions of their natures with the demands of God's Word. We can do this by a threefold program of:

(a) Memorizing God's Word to touch the mind (Ps. 119:9-11).

Our children should be encouraged not only to think about the truths of Scripture but also to commit God's Word to memory. A good way to do this is to decide on a verse of the week. During family devotions on Sunday, have one of the children write out the verse and place it in a prominent spot (e.g., on the refrigerator door). Review it every morning or evening at mealtime. Challenge one another to quote it on the spot during the week. Keep a book of memorized verses for periodic review. Be sure to choose verses that will be especially appropriate for your children and that are not too difficult for them to memorize. Even though they may be too young to understand the meaning of a verse, the Word that has been hidden away in their hearts can be brought back to their minds at any point by the power of the Holy Spirit (John 14:26).

Friends of ours tell the story of how their six-year-old son wandered off in a large shopping mall. When they finally located him, they discovered that he had comforted himself by quoting Joshua 1:9: "Have I not commanded you? Be strong and courageous! Do not tremble or be dismayed, for the Lord your God is with you wherever you go." He had memorized this verse at school just a few weeks earlier, and the Lord had enabled him to remember it at the appropriate time.

(b) Personalizing God's Word to touch the emotions (2 Sam. 12:7).

Scripture should never be taught to our children in a purely academic fashion. We must always seek to apply its principles and precepts to our children personally. It wasn't until Nathan said to David, "You are the man" that David repented of his sin of adultery.

One way we can do this is to take the verses we are having them memorize (or any verse of Scripture) and add personal pronouns whenever possible. For example, they could paraphrase Romans 3:23 to read, "For *I* have sinned and fall short of the glory of God." And they could read John 3:36 as, "If *I* believe in the Son, *I* have eternal life: but if *I* do not obey the Son, *I* shall not see life, but the wrath of God abides on *me*."

(c) Implementing God's Word to touch the will (James 4:17).

Not only should we encourage our children to memorize and personalize God's Word, but we should also urge them to put it to use by doing what it says. James 4:17 explains: "Therefore, to the one who knows the right thing to do, and does not do it, to him it is sin." Whether our children show evidence of a new heart or not, they must be encouraged to believe and obey God's Word. God's law has been written on their hearts so that even though they may not yet have been renewed by His Spirit, they are still held responsible to obey it (Rom. 2:14-15). As a Christian parent, therefore, I have always instructed my children to obey God's Word and trusted that as the Spirit was pleased to apply the Word to their hearts, they would recognize their spiritually bankrupt condition, acknowledge that they could not keep God's commandments, and then seek His forgiveness in Christ. I praise God that that is precisely what has happened to all three of my children.

In aiming for the heart, then, seek to apply God's Word to the mind, the emotions, and the will of your children. And most important of all, always be quick to take advantage of natural opportunities for presenting Christ as the solution to your children's needs.

3. *We must always assure our children of our unconditional love for them.* What was it about God's dealings with you that touched your heart most? For many of us it was the knowledge of God's great love for us—a love that moved Him to give His only Son for us while we were in total rebellion against Him (Rom. 5:8). In a similar way, our children need to know that we love them in spite of all their weaknesses and failures and sins. When they see that kind of love from us, they will be much more sensitive to the message of God's unconditional love for them. Their hearts will be more open to the Gospel when they are being brought up in a context of parental affection and acceptance that is secure and unchanging. In a later chapter we will look at this subject of unconditional love in greater detail.

4. *We must pray, pray, pray that God's Word will penetrate the hearts of our children.* If we really believe that "unless the Lord builds the house, they labor in vain who build it" (Ps. 127:1), then we must be diligent in calling upon His name for the salvation and spiritual growth of our children.

One of the primary stimuli for researching the subject of this book was the pain I felt at seeing several close friends and relatives reject the faith although they had been raised in Christian homes. For example, I think of my wife's cousin. As a senior in high school, Paul talked about becoming a pastor. But in his first year of college his inquisitive mind was overwhelmed with the intellectual arguments against

Christianity. He turned his back on the faith. In the years that followed I had several opportunities to talk with Paul about his doubts and problems with Christianity. He was open to talk but stubbornly refused to believe. All the while, however, Paul's godly parents, along with a host of other believers, prayed that he would return to the fold. The Lord answered our prayers some ten years and hundreds of prayers later. Today, praise God, Paul and his wife Linda are raising their three children in a Christian home.

Parents who pray faithfully for their sons and daughters, with the confidence that God in His mercy will save and keep them, need not be anxious. As Jesus said to the Canaanite woman who cried to Him for the healing of her demon-possessed daughter, so He says to parents who cry to Him for the spiritual healing of the children: "Your faith is great; be it done for you as you wish" (Matt. 15:28).

These four principles, then, are basic to our efforts of bringing the Gospel to bear on the hearts of our children. The question may be asked now, "How can we know when the Spirit is beginning to apply the truth to our children's hearts?" It is true that, like the wind, the Spirit "blows where He wills," (John 3:8) but we can at least look for certain rustlings in the leaves as evidence of His working in their inner beings.

LOOK FOR EVIDENCE OF THE SPIRIT'S WORK IN THE HEARTS OF OUR CHILDREN

As the Spirit of God takes our instruction and our example of the Christian life and causes them to be internalized and personally appropriated in our children's hearts, we should see three things begin to occur.

1. *Our children should become inquisitive about spiritual things.* It is true that children tend, by nature, to be inquisitive. But if God is truly at work in their hearts, we can expect their questions to focus more on matters of spiritual import (Ex. 12:26; Deut.6:20). For instance, when they ask why everyone can't eat and drink the elements at

the Lord's Supper, they may simply be hoping for a snack before they go home, or they may be beginning to understand that participation in the meal has something to do with one's relationship to Jesus.

2. *They will also display a sensitivity to spiritual concerns.* I'm sure you agree that one of the most distressing situations you will ever encounter as a Christian parent is observing in your child an attitude of indifference to the things of God. I know from firsthand experience, however, the joy that comes when God renews your child's heart. In each of my children I observed their indifference or mere toleration of spiritual things give way to serious thoughts about a right relationship with God. I saw them begin to spontaneously pursue spiritual activities, and I noticed that their ongoing battle with sin became a matter of great concern to them. Furthermore, as in the case of Samuel of old, they demonstrated a new openness to God's voice speaking through His Word (1 Sam. 3:10).

I can still remember the night my son, Brent, asked Christ to come into his life. In our devotions, we had been discussing the question of sin. He had been unusually attentive and visibly disturbed by the fact that his sin was deserving of hell. He asked question after question about sin, death, hell, and the Cross. It gave us a beautiful opportunity to present the simple Gospel message once again. Since Helen and I believe that God alone could save our children, we had resisted the temptation to pressure them into making a "decision for Jesus." But, at the same time, we were always looking for evidences that He was at work in their lives, wooing them to Himself. As much as we could discern that night, we believed God was drawing Brent into the kingdom. We were there simply to help steer him to the foot of the cross. I asked my son if he wanted to talk to God about the things we had been discussing. He said, "Yes," and in the simple prayer that followed he asked God to forgive him of all his sin and help him to love and serve Jesus. Brent was six years old when that happened.

Today, at twenty-one, he is still sensitive to spiritual things.

3. *Finally, our children will tend to be responsive to spiritual truth.* Sometimes we expect our children, upon confessing faith in Christ, to become perfect angels. The next time you are tempted to question the reality of your child's faith because of some expression of their remaining sin, take a good look at your own life. Remember, God has a lot of sanctifying work to do in both of you. What you should look for in your children, however, is a definite pattern of obedience to you and the commands of Scripture. If they do not exhibit a desire to be obedient, then they probably have not yet had a true change of heart.

Jeremiah 17:9 says, "The heart is more deceitful than all else and is desperately sick; who can understand it?" Only God truly sees and understands the nature of our children's hearts. He alone can infallibly discern whether or not their outward behavior is springing from a regenerate nature or a hypocritical one. Yet, He has clearly instructed us to aim for the hearts of our children as we communicate to them His life-changing Word. And, although inquisitiveness, sensitivity, and responsiveness to spiritual things may not be infallible signs that God is at work in their hearts, these outward signs certainly are grounds for believing parents to be encouraged and hopeful.

For Review, Discussion, and Action:

1. Based on the comments of Jesus in Matthew 15:1-9 define the word *hypocrisy.*

2. Give specific illustrations of how children can display a spirit of hypocrisy. Do you see any of these signs in your children?

3. Based on Proverbs 4:23; 21:2 and Romans 10:9-10, suggest three reasons why we should be concerned about touching the hearts of our children with the Gospel.

4. What are the four ways you can help bring God's Word to bear on the hearts of each of your children? Which of these activities are you presently pursuing?

5. Give specific illustrations of how you are presently appealing to the mind, emotions, and will of each of your children.

6. What three things should you look for in your children as an indication that their hearts have been touched by the Spirit of God?

7. Discuss what you should do as parents if you strongly suspect that your child is trying to play the part of a Christian when his/her heart is far from God?

For Further Study:

Chapin, Alice. *Building Your Child's Faith*. San Bernardino: Here's Life Publishers, Inc., 1983. Chapter 4 of this book, "A Child's Personal Decision for Christ," is of special value.

Haystead, Wes. *Teaching Your Children about God*. Ventura: Regal Books, 1974. This is an excellent book to help parents start training their children in the Christian Faith.

Inchley, John. *Kids and the Kingdom*. Wheaton: Tyndale House Publishers, Inc., 1976. This is a helpful book that gives a sound, biblically-based framework for the evangelization of children inside the church and outside the church.

Ingle, Clifford. *Children and Conversion*. Nashville: Broadman Press, 1970. This collection of ten papers was written by Baptist scholars on such subjects as "The

Child Within the Old Testament Community," "The Age of Accountability," and "Moral and Religious Growth."

Murray, Andrew. *How to Raise Your Children for Christ.* Minneapolis: Bethany Fellowship, Inc., 1975. This volume includes fifty-two insightful readings on how to raise your children in accordance with biblical principles and examples.

CHAPTER SIX

CREATE A CLIMATE OF UNCONDITIONAL LOVE

Faith-formation Principle: *To help our children come to an enduring faith in Christ, we must create an atmosphere of unconditional love in which the seeds of faith can germinate and grow in their hearts.*

Biblical Text: 1 Corinthians 13:1-8
It started out as a fun day. After all, I always looked forward to visiting my uncle's place. He operated a small service station in the tiny country village of Ethel, Ontario. On this particular Sunday afternoon, only my mother, my seventeen-year-old brother, and I had made the twenty-five mile trip; my father, a pharmacist, had to work.

About mid-afternoon my cousin and I were playing in my father's car. I decided it was time to demonstrate how well I could drive at the age of ten. I started the car, slipped it into gear, and began to let out the clutch. As the car jerked forward, I aimed for the opening between the gas pump and the back of a nearby tractor. CRUNCH! Nobody had told me that tractors have long hitches protruding beyond their back tires. This hitch carved a deep slice, fifteen inches long, in the passenger side front door.

The trip home was an extremely quiet one. I felt very, very sick inside. My father had told me never to turn on the ignition of a car. I had disobeyed him, and I was sure he would never forgive me for what I had done. I could never forgive myself. I guess my father knew that because later that night, after I had fearfully and tearfully apologized, he took me aside, and we had a long father-to-son chat. He let me know he was *very* unhappy about what I had done, and we discussed what would be appropriate punishment (I think the punishment was a combination of being grounded for a period of time and giving up my meager allowance for the same amount of time). But the part I remember most clearly is when he put his arm around me, said "I forgive you," and then reassured me that no damaged car door would ever stop him from loving me.

I can't say I slept well that night, but I can say that if I had ever before doubted my father's love for me, I never doubted it again. And furthermore, my love for him and my desire to obey him grew immensely that day.

Unconditional love. We hear a lot about it. Child psychologists tell us we should love our children unconditionally. Of course, as Christians we know that that is the kind of love God has demonstrated to us in Christ. But what is unconditional love? And how can we show it to our children without at the same time providing them with an opportunity to take advantage of us? What does unconditional love have to do with faith development in their lives? These are the questions we hope to answer in this chapter.

CREATE A CLIMATE THAT FOSTERS SPIRITUAL RECEPTIVITY

I purposely used the word *climate* in the title of this chapter because the word speaks of the atmosphere in which our children are raised in the faith. The environment of some Christian homes reminds me of a military camp where orders are barked from morning to night; others are like a busy day on Wall Street—noisy, chaotic, and competitive. But the best atmosphere or climate for developing the seeds of saving faith is the one characterized by unconditional love.

When I speak of an atmosphere or climate of unconditional love, I have in mind not only the specific things we say and do to express our love but also the attitudes which generate those loving actions. Unfortunately, our intended acts of love can be misinterpreted by our children if they do not sense an attitude of love and acceptance behind our words and deeds. Let me try to illustrate what I mean from Paul's comments on true love in 1 Corinthians 13.

The apostle begins his discussion of true love by mentioning several activities that some people may view as acceptable substitutes:

● *Speaking in tongues of men and angels* (v. 1). This is a reference to powers of both earthly and heavenly utterances.

● *Exercising the gift of prophecy and understanding mysteries and knowledge* (v. 2). This refers to the ability to know God's will in all things and to possess all human wisdom and discernment.

● *Possessing all faith* (v. 2). Here, the reference concerns a special gift of miraculous faith—faith in its fullest measure.

● *Delivering our own body to be burned, and giving our possessions to the poor* (v. 3). This is a reference to acts of great sacrifice and self-denial in the interests of others.

All of these actions are commendable; however, the whole point of the apostle's argument is that if these activities are not motivated by an attitude of true love, they are of no profit to anyone. This is true of the relationship between parents and their children too. For example, consider the case of the father who barks orders to his children morning, noon, and night. They obey him but, because there is no expression of love in the use of his tongue, they do not enjoy being around him. I have met many well-educated parents who could impress their children with their great knowledge of the world around them and could teach them all of God's will, but because they did not love them unconditionally, they ultimately lost the respect of their children. Even parents who demonstrate great faith in God and a life of personal sacrifice for others will make little lasting impression on their children if they fail to communicate real love to them. How many pastors or missionaries have been pained by the bitter cry of an angry child, "You always had time for other people but no time for me."

I have had distressed parents sit in my study and in tears ask me, "What went wrong? We taught them the Word of God. We gave them knowledge of the faith. We believed God for their salvation. We were always willing to make great personal sacrifices for our kids. Why have they turned away from the Lord?" The answer is not always the same, but in many cases the basic problem has been the parents' failure to communicate an attitude of unconditional love to their children.

Notice I did not say these parents failed to love their kids. Everything they told me they had done for their children was prompted by their love for them. It's a rare parent who does not love his children more than his own life. The problem most of us have is in communicating that love to our children so that they are assured of it. We think they should automatically view our teaching of them, providing for their needs, and making sacrifices for them as expressions of our affection. But, more often than not, they simply view those things as our natural, parental responsibilities. And perhaps they are right. Somehow we must convey that our actions really are prompted by love. Our children must be made to *feel* that we love them. They must sense the *climate* of unconditional love.

In his book *How to Really Love Your Child* Dr. Ross Campbell writes:

> Emotionality and spirituality are not entirely separate entities. One is quite related to and dependent upon the other. For this reason, if parents want to help a child spiritually, they must care for him first emotionally. Because a child remembers feelings more easily than facts, there must be a series of pleasant memories upon which to accumulate the facts, especially spiritual facts.[1]

The preceding quotation suggests two points of special importance to parents. First, we must consider the relationship between a child's emotional stability and his spiritual receptivity. Dr. Campbell implies that if children have happy experiences in their childhood, they will be more open to consider the claims of the Gospel. If children feel loved by their parents, they will be more able to appreciate God's love as displayed in Christ. Second, Dr. Campbell states that by nature small children are more emotive than cognitive. That is, they can remember how they felt about a particular situation much better than they can remember the facts of the situation itself. This means that unless our children feel loved, they may not be as open to considering or remembering the facts of the Gospel as we seek to instruct them. If the climate in our home is not one in which an attitude of love prevails, then the seeds of faith may never take root.

Although the apostle does not use the term *unconditional love* in 1 Corinthians 13:4ff., that's the kind of love he has in mind. He does not say, "Love is patient unless your children are bickering with one another at a time when you have a bad headache and are trying to get supper ready for the guests." Nor does he say, "Love is kind, except when you return home after a particularly hard day at work only to be told as you come through the front door that you have to go and pick up your son at basketball practice." There are no conditions attached to true, *agape* love. "Love," says Paul, "bears *all* things, believes *all* things, hopes *all* things, endures *all* things" (v. 7, emphasis added). It is this kind of unconditional love that "never fails," even with our children (v. 8).

Our parental expressions of unconditional love are the greatest illustrations our children can have of God's unconditional love for them. When children are nurtured in that kind of love by their parents, it is much easier for them to comprehend and accept the Heavenly Father's unconditional love in Christ. In fact, the way our Father above displays His love for us is the pattern of love we should emulate in our dealings with our children.

REFLECT GOD'S UNCONDITIONAL LOVE

If you had to name one specific aspect of the Gospel message that was most instrumental in drawing you to faith in Christ, what would it be? I'm sure many of us were drawn to Christ by the amazing truth of God's unconditional love for us. That kind of love, a love so great that He gave His only Son (John 3:16), captures people's attention, challenges their minds, and touches their hearts. In short, it is God's irresistible magnet to draw men to Himself (John 12:32). But that same kind of love, when incarnated in the lives of Christian parents, can be used by God to draw our children to Him.

If we are to reflect unconditional love to our children, we must imitate our Father's love in at least three ways.

1. *We must accept our children just as God made them.* When God adds individuals to His body, He does not do so on the basis of their I.Q., personality, natural talents, athletic abilities, physical appearance, or any other personal qualities. He chooses us simply because He loves us (Eph. 1:4-5). He accepts us just as He made us, defects and all. That is precisely how we are to love our children.

Unfortunately, some parents, especially fathers, tend to measure the worth of their children on how well they succeed in this world. After all, that's how the world measures success today, isn't it—by how well you do at college, how fast you climb the corporate ladder, how big a name you make for yourself in your particular field? It shouldn't surprise us, then, that some of us can also begin to view our children's value by a similar false standard. When we do this, however, the message we communicate to the children is: "The higher the grades, the more I love you" or, "The more you succeed in sports or music or your job, the more proud I am to be your parent" or, "The prettier you look or the more you watch your diet, the more I accept you."

Now, maybe you are saying to yourself, "I would never say those things to my children." I hope you wouldn't, because those words would clearly send your children a message of *conditional* love. We all must be careful not to convey an attitude of rejection by the expectations we place on our children. We can communicate conditional love to our children without even knowing we are doing it. For example, when we criticize them in public because we are embarrassed by what they are wearing or how they are behaving, we are sending messages that we are ashamed of them and that we will love them only if they look and act a certain way. I'm not saying we must never register our dismay or concern over such things; I'm simply saying we should be careful when, where, and how we do it. If Jesus tells us we should go to our brother in secret in order to confront him with his sin (Matt. 18:15), then surely we can treat our children with the same respect.

Remember the text of our second chapter, Proverbs 22:6: "Train up a child in the way he should go, even when he is old he will not depart from it"? We discussed that what Solomon was really saying was, "Train up a child according to his own way, that is, according to the unique way that God has made him." Don't measure your child's intellectual abilities against the standard achieved by your other children. Don't expect all your children to excel at sports because your first son was a natural athlete. God has made each of your children different, but He loves each one unconditionally. And so must you.

During our nearly twenty years of parenting, Helen and I have required basically two things of our children. We have always told them that we expect them to do their best and to do what God's Word requires of them. They may not win the trophy or get straight *A's*, but if they do their best and seek to please the Lord, that is all we expect. Within the limits of these two broad guidelines, we have found that our three children have plenty of room to display their individual personalities, sense of creativity, and unique abilities.

In his excellent book, *How to Keep Your Kids on Your Team*, Dr. Charles Stanley makes an interesting point about demonstrating unconditional love to our children:

> It is important for you as a parent to make a distinction between individuality, creativity and rebellion. I have seen many cases in which a child's creativity and individuality have been misunderstood as rebellion. . . . In an attempt to "deliver" them from something we see as potentially harmful, we sometimes take away avenues through which they can legitimately express their God-given creativity. When parents do this, children usually interpret it as rejection.[2]

Unconditional love sometimes requires that we allow our children to pursue a course with which we may be uncomfortable. For example, when our son was in tenth grade, he began working a few hours every night for a janitorial company, cleaning offices in a nearby industrial complex. At first, his mother and I had mixed emotions about the job because we were concerned about it affecting his performance at school. We knew, however, that Brent had always been a hard worker, self-disciplined, and able to keep his priorities in order, so we complied with his wishes. Today, as he enters his third year of college, he still has this part-time janitorial job, but now he is a supervisor, training the new recruits. He has discovered and developed administrative skills he never knew he had, and he has learned to be a wise steward of his money. Much to our delight he has also paid his own college tuition thus far. If we had refused to allow our son to take that job, he would have missed out on these positive benefits. What is worse, he might have decided our refusal to trust his judgment on the matter meant we did not love and respect him, and he might have ended up resenting us for it. Unconditional love requires accepting our children just as God made them. And sometimes that means viewing our children's requests to pursue a particular course, not as an expression of rebellion or as a desire to be different, but simply as a natural expression of their unique, God-given abilities and interests.

2. *We must accept our children with all of their sins and rebellious tendencies.* God, in His unconditional love, not only accepted us as He made us, but He also received us in all of our sinful pride, stubbornness, and weakness. In Romans 5:8 we read: "God demonstrates His own love toward us, in that while we were yet sinners, Christ died for us." His love for us did not lead Him to minimize or ignore our sin; it led Him to take positive action to help us overcome our sin problem. God so loved that He gave. Do we so love our children, even when they are most clearly expressing their sinful natures, that we determine to give ourselves to bringing them up in the nurture and admonition of the Lord? One thing is certain, we cannot just look the other way and ignore our children's sin and sinful behavior.

We are told in Job 1:5 that every morning Job offered burnt sacrifices for his sons perchance they had "sinned and cursed God in their hearts." Of course today we don't have to offer redemptive sacrifices for our children when they sin; however, we can love them unconditionally by giving ourselves to them in other ways. We can love them by praying regularly that God will be at work in their hearts convicting them of sin and drawing them to Himself for salvation. Let's be honest, parents—praying for our children on a daily basis calls for self-discipline and self-sacrifice. It demands *agape* love. We also demonstrate love to our children by dealing properly with their sinful behavior. Only loving parents will take time to pray with disobedient children and teach them that God is willing to forgive sinners who come to Him through faith in Christ's work on the Cross. And, of course, another way we as parents exhibit unconditional love is to forgive our children willingly when they have sinned against us.

At every stage of our children's development they will display certain habits or behavior patterns that are not sinfully motivated at all, but are nonetheless offensive or irritating to us. At such times we must learn to "cover over with love" (1 Peter 4:8). To treat the whining of a three-year-old or the clumsiness of an adolescent as gross sins is a big mistake. Discipline for these things confuses our children because their behavior is quite normal for them at that age; it may also lessen the parent's effectiveness in dealing with real sinful behavior. Furthermore, disciplining for such behavior could lead to such confusion and bitterness that our children will ultimately give up trying to please either their parents or God—"I get yelled at no matter what I do, so why bother?" When our children consistently feel that way, it is likely that we have exasperated them to the point that they have lost heart and probably even rejected us and the faith (Col. 3:21; Eph. 6:4). So unconditional love requires finding a way to accept and deal with our children in all of their sins and offensive habits.

3. *We must not hesitate to administer loving discipline when it is called for.* Some parents may think they are expressing unconditional love by holding back discipline,

but they will probably live to regret their decision. In Hebrews 12 we have a detailed description of how God disciplines His people. The whole point of the passage is that this divine discipline is an expression of God's paternal love for us. In Hebrews 12:6, the author quotes Solomon's advice to his son in Proverbs 3:12: "For those whom the Lord loves He disciplines, and He scourges every son whom He receives." Let there be no mistake. When discipline is called for, the path of unconditional love is not to give a Dr. Spock smile and look the other way, but rather to discipline "as seems best" (Heb. 12:10).

When our children are small, and we know they have done something that calls for the rod or some other form of correction or punishment (we will discuss these things more in chapter 11), we must not be influenced by their tears or pleadings or wailings to turn away from the path of discipline (Prov. 23:13-14). Remember, it's unconditional love that we are expressing. In this case, not even the conditions of pain (theirs or ours) or inconvenience (ours) must prevent us from diligent follow-through. As the author of Hebrews puts it:

> All discipline for the moment seems not to be joyful, but sorrowful; yet to those who have been trained by it, afterwards it yields the peaceful fruit of righteousness. Therefore, strengthen the hands that are weak and the knees that are feeble (Heb. 12:11-12).

Parents, we need to apply this truth, not only to God's dealings with us, but also to our dealings with our children. If we really love them unconditionally, we will strengthen our weak hands and knees by administering the appropriate discipline, even though we know it will cause sorrow and not joy. Why do we do it? Because in the end discipline will cause them to produce the "peaceful fruit of righteousness" (v. 11). It will be one of the means by which the Lord will bring our children to an abiding faith in Him.

The Apostle John wrote, "Beloved (parents), if God so loved us (unconditionally), we also ought to love one another (our children)." This Spackman, amplified translation of 1 John 4:11 best summarizes what I have been stressing in this chapter. Unconditional love, as defined in 1 Corinthians 13, is to be the climate in which we raise our family because such a climate reflects the way God deals with sinners in order to draw them to Himself.

For Review, Discussion, and Action:

1. What do we mean when we speak about providing a *climate* of unconditional love in the home?

2. What implications does 1 Corinthians 13:1-3 have for dealing with our children in terms of unconditional love?

3. Because small children are more feeling-oriented than fact-oriented, in what ways are you seeking to ensure that your children feel your unconditional love?

4. Give a specific illustration of how you would demonstrate unconditional love to your children according to each of the specific qualities listed in 1 Corinthians 13:4-7. (For example, "I will unconditionally love my children by being *patient* with them when they forget to clean the mud off their feet before coming into the house.)

5. Discuss three specific ways God's love for us sets the pattern for loving our children unconditionally. How well are you demonstrating each of these qualities of love to your children? Which one do you need to work on the most?

6. Ask each of your children what they think they have to do to make you proud of them.

For Further Study:

Campbell, Ross. *How to Really Love Your Child.* Wheaton: Victor Books, 1977. This popular book deals with ways to express love to our children through physical touch, positive eye contact, and focused attention.

Campbell, Ross. *How to Really Love Your Teenager.* Wheaton: Victor Books, 1981. This book is similar to Dr. Campbell's earlier book but aimed at dealing with teens. The author focuses on unconditional love in chapter 3.

Herring, Reuben and Dorothy. *Becoming Friends with Your Children.* Nashville: Broadman Press, 1984. Written primarily to help parents develop a friendship with their children that will last throughout all their days, this book deals with the subject of parental love in chapter 4.

McLean, Gordon. *What's a Parent to Do?* Wheaton: Victor Books, 1983. This book concentrates primarily on how parents should handle the serious problems facing their teenage children today (sex, drugs, etc.). Chapter 4 deals with parental love.

Stanley, Charles. *How to Keep Your Kids on Your Team.* Nashville: Oliver Nelson Books, 1986. Stanley has written one of the best books I've read on how to keep your kids in the faith. See chapter 4 for a discussion on unconditional love.

CHAPTER SEVEN

STOP, LOOK, AND LISTEN

Faith-formation Principle: *To help our children come to an enduring faith in Christ, we must learn how to maintain open communication with them when our anger threatens to become a stumbling block to their interest in the Faith.*

Biblical Text: James 1:19-20

I am convinced that we make some of the deepest impressions on the minds of our children when we deal with them in anger. As I think back on my own childhood, I have mostly good memories. My parents loved the Lord and were very active in the church and in Christian organizations such as the Gideons and Christian Businessmen International. During my high school days, Dad sponsored the Inter-School Christian Fellowship group in our local high school. I was proud of my father and had a good relationship with him and my mom.

One painful experience that I do remember, however, occurred when I was about fourteen or fifteen. My mom, dad, and I were vacationing with my aunt and cousin in Montreal, Quebec. We had been touring the large cathedral on Mount Royale and were heading back to the motel for a rest. My dad was complaining of a bad headache. As we left the parking lot, my father turned right and headed up a side street. I said, "Dad, I think this takes us back up to the top of the hill. It dead-ends at the cathedral." (During our tour I had observed several cars that were forced to turn around at the end of this street). My father ignored my continued warnings until he came to the dead end. At that point I boastfully said, "See, I told you so! I knew it was a dead end. I was right. Why didn't you listen to me?"

I can't remember everything my father said in response to my less-than-diplomatic (or respectful) words. But I do remember one thing. He said, "Don't you *ever* say, 'I told you so,' to me again." And I remember his anger. He simply exploded. I was devastated because I knew I had embarrassed and hurt my father deeply, and I knew I was wrong in the way I had spoken to him. I apologized as soon as we got back to the motel, and he forgave me. But that one brief incident, for me, and I suspect for my father too, cast a shadow over the rest of the vacation.

The main point of this personal illustration is that words spoken in a moment of anger can make lasting impressions on our children. In my case, my father's outburst of anger was out of character. Furthermore, I was old enough to realize that I was at fault and, in a sense, deserved what I got. Also, my relationship with my father was quickly restored. But the fact remains that I still remember the incident with sadness some thirty-two years after it happened.

Imagine, then, what kinds of impressions can be made on the minds and emotions of sensitive, young children who, throughout their entire childhood, are barraged by angry words and behavior. Some of you reading this book may still be carrying around emotional hurts and scars because of words your parents said to you in anger. Do you want your children to have a similar legacy? Of course not. Then I urge you to pay careful attention to the content of this chapter and the one to follow.

Much has been written, from both a Christian and a non-Christian point of view, about anger and how to control it. My remarks on the subject are restricted primarily to the relationship between parental anger and children who reject the faith. I am convinced that an angry tongue can become the devil's tool, not only to destroy communication between parents and their children, but also to discourage children from seriously considering the Christian faith.

BE SLOW TO ANGER

There are basically two kinds of anger—constructive and destructive. Righteous indignation is constructive anger. It is not the kind of anger that is aroused by injustice or hurt done to one's own person. Rather, it is anger that is prompted by a zeal for righteousness and truth and the glory of God. It is anger that discharges its energy by identifying with righteous activities and constructive causes. Some of us get very angry when we hear of doctors lining their own pockets by murdering unborn infants. This is righteous indignation. It leads us to righteous actions such as writing letters to congressmen, participating in protest marches at hospitals and abortion clinics, and opening our homes to unwed mothers and their babies.

As parents, we can experience righteous indignation over our children's sinful disobedience. For instance, have you ever had the experience of telling your child to stop doing something, only to have him look you straight in the eyes, give a defiant "No!" and continue to disobey you? I'm sure you have. Such conduct is clearly an expression of your child's sinful, rebellious heart. And we shouldn't be surprised if we sense a feeling of anger in situations like this. As long as our anger leads us to seek constructive ways to deal with their unacceptable behavior, it remains righteous indignation. When we lose self-control or just strike out at our children with punishment that is totally unfair or devoid of any desire for their ultimate well-being, we have given in to destructive anger.

We must remember that the line between righteous anger and sinful anger is a very fine line. The emotion of anger itself is a very deceiving emotion. It is so all-consuming that it quickly clouds our judgment, silences the voice of reason, blocks out the conscience, and opens the door for sinful thoughts and actions. That is precisely why James says, "Be slow to anger" (James 1:19).

Someone has said, "It becomes us to be zealous for God's cause, cool for our own." This distinction is probably most difficult to maintain when it comes to raising our children. When their sinful conduct evokes anger in our hearts, we are not always clear as to whether we should be "zealous for God's cause" or "cool for our own."

BE WILLING TO CONFESS YOUR SINFUL ANGER

The Apostle James sees a relationship between the believer's ability to control his anger and the achieving of the righteousness of God: "This you know, my beloved brethren. But let everyone be quick to hear, slow to speak and slow to anger; for the anger of man does not achieve the righteousness of God" (James 1:19-20). But what exactly does he mean when he says, "the anger of man does not achieve the righteousness of God"? There are two possible ways to interpret this statement.

1. *Paul could be saying that anger (i.e., sinful anger) does not reflect the righteousness of God.* In other words, angry people don't generally do righteous deeds; they do sinful ones. Their anger inhibits any desire they may have had for doing the right or righteous thing. They just react impulsively.

2. *He could mean that the anger of man does not promote a love of righteousness in our own lives or in the lives of other people, namely those who observe the anger or are the direct objects of it* . For parents this means that when we are sinfully angry with our children, we are not only acting contrary to the righteousness of God in our own lives, but we are also discouraging its development in

the lives our children. To put it bluntly, by modeling an
angry spirit, we are telling our children that it is all right to
become sinfully angry. We are gradually destroying a love
of righteousness in their hearts and, ultimately, we could
drive them away from the faith. This ought to be an extremely sobering fact for parents.

I am not suggesting that if you have been sinfully angry
with your children (and what parent hasn't?) that you may
have lost them from the faith, and you no longer have any
hope of winning them to Christ. Periodic outbursts of anger are part of every normal family, including Christian
families. But the important question for you as a parent is:
"How do I handle my sinful anger?" Do you ignore it and
hope the kids will forget how you acted? Do you explain it
away by saying, "I'm the parent, I can do as I please"? Or
do you do the right thing and ask forgiveness of your children when you've been sinfully angry with them? I can
testify from firsthand experience that children are very forgiving. They are resilient individuals who can bounce back
from the hurt of an unkind word or an unfair punishment if
they know Dad and Mom are genuinely sorry for what they
did.

Not only will you find that your children will forgive you,
but you will also find that such occasions provide natural
opportunities to talk to them about God's willingness to
forgive them. Most Christian parents are able to forgive
their children when they ask forgiveness for an act of disobedience, but I have found surprisingly few parents who
are quick to apologize to their children when they know
they have sinned against them. One man told me, "I could
never admit to my child I was wrong. He would never
respect me as a parent if I did that." That man was wrong.
And what is worse, by refusing to admit his own sinful
weaknesses, he lost many ideal situations to teach his child
about the forgiving grace of God.

When we know we have lost our cool by becoming sinfully angry with our children, we must make sure that we

have reconciled with them before they go to bed at night. When Paul says, "Don't let the sun go down on your wrath," the word he uses for *wrath* is the same one he uses in Ephesians 6:4 when he says, "Fathers, do not *provoke* your children to anger." So he's saying, "Don't go to bed provoked at anyone, including your children. It will harm both you and them."

I've had some of the best discussions with my children when I've had to tell them I was sorry for the way I acted. I remember one occasion, in particular, when I really blew it in the discipline of my son. I had spanked him for something which, I discovered later, he had not done. When I realized my mistake, I went to him in his room and said, "Brent, I must ask your forgiveness for the way I disciplined you. I was angry with you and did not listen to your explanation of what happened. Your mother told me you were telling the truth. I am sorry I did not trust your word. I was the one who sinned in this case, and I've asked God to forgive me, but I must ask you to forgive me too. Would you please forgive me?" He did, and then we both prayed together and asked God to help us both be more true to Him.

There is something about making yourself open and vulnerable to your children that makes them more vulnerable to you. And they become more open to the Gospel message. This is true whether the situation calls for them to forgive you, or you to forgive them, or both of you to forgive each other. Our children develop a heightened sensitivity to spiritual things whenever we are willing to come to them and "settle before sunset."

I am convinced that what our children need most is not perfect parents but parents who know how to stand at the foot of the cross with their children. Parents who give the impression that they never sin will not impress their children; they will discourage and maybe even intimidate them. But parents who are totally honest with their children, admitting to ongoing struggles with sin and their need for

God's forgiveness, will find their children following this parental example. These children will learn to acknowledge their own sin and, hopefully, they will also turn to Christ for the solution to their sin problem.

If we are faithful to humble ourselves and follow God's prescribed way of reconciliation, the righteousness of God can be achieved in our children's lives, even when there have been times of sinful anger.

BE WILLING TO STOP, LOOK, AND LISTEN

Most of us have heard the little safety jingle, "Stop, look, and listen before you cross the street." I would like to revise that to say, "Stop, look, and listen before you begin to speak." That is basically what James 1:19 instructs us to do: "Be quick to hear [listen], slow to speak and slow to anger." Listening to children is not a natural talent for most parents. It is especially difficult to listen to them when their behavior has begun to stir up our anger. But God's Word is clear—we must learn to stop, look, and listen before we begin to speak.

Maybe you think, "Well, I've always believed that children are to be seen and not heard." Who says so? God? I don't know of any place in the Scriptures where children are told to keep quiet in the home. Let's be honest—we tend to think that because we are the parents (and therefore, older, wiser, and bigger), we alone have a right to speak. We can speak about anything we want, when we want, as long as we want, and as loudly as we want. We even feel we have the right to interrupt our children whenever we desire.

When we act like that, what we are saying to our children is: "What you think or what you have to say on the subject is not important. Your opinion doesn't count." I'm sure most of us do not really feel that way about our children, but we convey such a message to them when we consistently refuse to let them speak. As we have said in previous chapters, children can sense the attitude behind our words and actions. They know whether or not we are showing a genuine concern for them. When we do not allow them to speak, or when they sense we are not really listening to them as they speak, they may very well conclude that they are not important to us.

So often we forget that the problems of our children, which may seem insignificant to us, are major concerns for them. "After all," we say to ourselves, "how can a broken bicycle wheel, or a spelling quiz at the end of the week, or unkind remarks by the kids at school, be as important as earning enough money to pay the mortgage, or finding transportation to work when the car is out of commission?" Well, our children's problems seem just as big to them as ours seem to us. Furthermore, they do not have years of experience to lean on in handling problems, as you and I do. Surely then, we can give our children the freedom and the encouragement to share with us how they feel about their concerns. Surely we can take the time to let them give their own explanation of why they behaved the way they did. Even when our children are young and just learning to express themselves, we should learn to "stop, look, and listen" to them—especially when we are becoming angry over their behavior. We must be slow to anger and slow to speak, but quick to hear.

Let's think for a moment how this would work in a real-life situation. Your child comes to you in tears and interrupts you at the most exciting part of the book you are reading or the TV program you are watching. You have overheard bits and pieces of the argument he has been having with his sister in the next room, and your tolerance level has already reached the simmering point. You know you should have done something sooner, but you were either too lazy or too involved in what you were doing to break away and settle the dispute in its earlier stages. You had hoped that maybe a miracle would occur and the two of them would realize how sinfully they were acting, break down in tears, and go rushing into one another's arms pleading for forgiveness. But it didn't happen that way. It never does. And so here you are again, having to deal with what seems to be a no-win situation. What do you do when everything within you says, "Scream!"

Stop! Stop what you are doing—put down the book or get up from the TV or the computer or the dishes. You say by that very action, "Your problem is important to me, more important than what I am currently doing."

Look! Look straight into your child's eyes. Don't stare at the floor or out the window. For small children especially, it is your eye contact that tells them you are really paying attention. They can't read your mind, but they can sense your attentive spirit if they see you looking at them. So maintain good eye contact.

Listen! Listen whether you want to or not. Listen whether you believe it's the truth or a lie. Listen! And don't interrupt your child when he is speaking unless it is to ask clarifying questions, or to rephrase what he just said so that you understand him better (Prov. 18:13).

Stop, look, and listen! Be quick to hear but slow to speak and slow to anger. If you can learn to do this in every situation, you will not only learn more facts before you act, but you will have time to cool down and to give more thought to a just settlement of the problem. If your children know they will be heard and not just told to keep their mouths shut and listen, I believe you will have more contented children. And you will develop a closer relationship with them.

LISTEN AND ENCOURAGE FAITH ACCEPTANCE

If you do not learn to listen to your children, you will soon discourage them from ever expressing opinions or feelings. By the time they reach adolescence, you will wonder why they never speak to you, never share their hurts and fears with you, and never ask you for your ideas on things. They just shut themselves away in their room or seek out others for a listening ear.

Worse yet, by not having an open ear to your children, you may be driving them away from the faith. A child may reason, "If my parents don't care about what I think or how I feel, then how can I be sure God cares?" For any of our children to come to that conclusion would be tragic. The fact is, the God of the Bible is very eager to listen to us. He tells us to come to Him and express our thoughts freely to Him. In Isaiah 1:18 He says, "Come now, and let us reason together." In Isaiah 43:26 He says, "Put Me in remembrance; let us argue our case together, state your cause that you may be proved right."

If the God of heaven and earth is eager to hear us, reason with us, and sympathize with us, then surely we can learn to develop the same attitude toward our children. I am so grateful to the Lord that, in His anger, He showed me mercy. I am so thankful that He still deals patiently with me, is attentive to my needs, and is always open to my approaching Him. If He can "stop, look, and listen" to me, then I can certainly do the same for my children.

In the Youth Congress '85 survey, referred to in chapter 3, I discovered that 33 percent of those teens who claimed to have parents who listened to them had considered rejecting the faith. Of those teens who felt their parents did not listen to them, 49 percent said they had considered rejecting the faith. Similar statistics were true of those who said they had forsaken the faith for a time. Thirty-seven percent of that group claimed to have parents who were good listeners while 48 percent of them claimed to have parents who were poor listeners. So the statistics support the fact that when we allow our children to speak and when we attentively listen to them, they are more likely to come to an abiding faith in Christ.

If we learn to keep the lines of communication open with our children even when we are angry with them, we will not become a stumbling block to their faith in God. We must also learn the difference between destructive and constructive anger. We must never let sinful anger stand between us and our children. Sinful anger, in us or in our children, will leave the door open for Satan to strengthen his grip on their lives and drive them further away from the faith. We must instead model a spirit of patience and self-control. Our example will exert a positive influence in their lives which, by God's grace, will help to achieve the righteousness of God in them.

For Review, Discussion, and Action:

1. Define and discuss two kinds of anger. Give illustrations of each kind of anger from Scripture and from your own life.

2. What are the two possible interpretations of James 1:20: "The anger of man does not achieve the righteousness of God"?

3. What should you do when you know you have been sinfully angry with your child? How can you turn this experience into a positive spiritual blessing for your child? What obstacles in your life would make it difficult for you to ask your child for forgiveness?

4. What does the phrase "stop, look, and listen before you begin to speak" mean? Discuss some practical situations when this advice would help you deal with your children.

5. Discuss the potential effects on our children if we encourage them to speak and then listen to them. How will our children be affected if we do not allow them to speak or don't listen when they are speaking?

6. How do you think your children would rate you as a listener—poor, fair, or good? Ask each of your children to rate you. If necessary, ask them for forgiveness and pray with them for God's help in becoming a good listener.

For Further Study:

Adams, Jay E. *The Christian Counselor's Manual.* Phillipsburg: Presbyterian and Reformed Publishing Company, 1973. On pages 348–367, Dr. Adams gives helpful directives on how to handle sinful anger.

Campbell, Ross. *How to Really Love Your Teenager.* Wheaton: Victor Books, 1984. Dr. Campbell touches on parental anger in chapter 6 where he deals with how to maintain self-control.

Mack, Wayne. *A Homework Manual for Biblical Counselors.* Vol. 1. Phillipsburg: Presbyterian and Reformed Publishing Company, 1979. The first two sections in this manual provide numerous questions designed to help the reader find biblical solutions to the problem of anger.

Ridenour, Fritz. *What Teenagers Wish Their Parents Knew about Kids.* Waco: Word Books, 1982. In chapter 6, Ridenour has some helpful ideas on how to be an active listener to your children. In chapter 7, entitled "Anger, the Enemy Within," Ridenour defines anger and its causes (fear, hurt, and frustration) and then describes and analyzes an angry exchange he had with his son.

CHAPTER EIGHT

BUILD UP, DON'T TEAR DOWN

Faith-formation Principle: To help our children come to an enduring faith in Christ, we must help them develop a healthy level of self-worth by treating them with respect and by speaking words that build them up and minister grace to them.

Biblical Text: Ephesians 4:29

One of the most thorough studies of American church youth in recent years was conducted by Merton P. Strommen, president of Youth Research Center. Between the years 1970 and 1977 he gave a 420-item survey to over 21,000 teens between the ages of 14 and 18. In his book, *Five Cries of Youth*, Strommen sets forth the interesting results of his investigation. He discusses:

(1) The cry of self-hatred (low self-esteem)
(2) The cry of psychological orphans (family tensions)
(3) The cry of social protest (concern over lack of social conscience)
(4) The cry of the prejudiced (repulsion by hypocrisy)
(5) The cry of the joyous (hope and sense of identity for those in Christ).

The cries ... challenge the adequacy of a youth
ministry that is all evangelism, all social involvement, all socializing activities, or all doctrinal instruction. They posit five basic needs or value ori-
entations, requiring five distinct accents in a youth
ministry.[1]

I wholeheartedly agree with Strommen's concern that
youth ministries (and parents) must focus on these needs
of our youth. Of special interest for us in this chapter is the
first cry, the cry of self-hatred.

RECOGNIZE YOUR CHILD'S WORTH

Much has been written over the past two decades about
the importance of developing a positive self-image or sense
of self-esteem in our children. Unfortunately, not much of
this material has been based on a truly biblical definition of
self-worth. Of the few Christian authors who do deal with
the appropriate Scriptures, not all believe that the building
of a good self-image is a prerequisite to healthy relationships with others.[2] They argue that it is only when we
realize who we are, or can be, in Christ that we can really
have a sense of true self-worth. In other words, our children need to come to a personal knowledge of God's love
for them before they can experience biblical self-identity. I
fully agree with this application of the Scriptures.

Does this mean that until our children show evidence of
new life in Christ, we can do nothing to help them develop
a healthy attitude of self-worth? Of course not. When I
think of self-image or self-regard, I think of the degree to
which one accepts himself as a person of value and potential. As Christian parents, we are in a privileged position to
provide the kind of firm foundation necessary for the development of a truly healthy self-image in our children.
Consider the following statements.

1. *Our children have worth because they are created in
our image.* They are *our* children. They are born with

something of each of their parents in them. As they grow up under our care, our children draw from us biologically, intellectually, psychologically, socially, and spiritually. They are extensions of ourselves and reflections of who we are. If, therefore, we have any sense of personal self-worth, we should naturally regard our children as having a similar value.

An increasing number of Christian families are adopting children. Are these children of any less value than natural children? Absolutely not! Not only do they have value by virtue of the traits inherited from their biological parents, but they also have the additional blessing of being especially chosen by God to be placed into a Christian home. In every respect, apart from their biological origin, they become as much a part of their new family as do children who are born into it.

2. *Our children have worth because they are made in the image of God.* They are not, as the behaviorists tell us, sophisticated animals. They are creatures endowed with many of the attributes that are found in the Creator Himself. The fact that the divine image is grossly distorted and marred by their sinful nature does not eliminate their worth or their worthiness of our respect. They have an inalienable birthright to be treated with dignity and to view themselves as having value.

3. *Our children have worth because they are living within the sphere of Gospel influence.* I discussed this idea in chapter 1 when I referred to 1 Corinthians 7:14 in which Paul says the children of believers are "holy." In that chapter we discussed that this word, *holy,* means at the very least that God has shown His special favor to our children by giving them believing parents and thereby placing them in a position where they receive a more consistent exposure to a Gospel witness than do other children. This, I believe, should be communicated to our children—not to encourage them to regard themselves as believers, but to help them understand their unique privilege and responsi-

bility to believe in Christ. Living within the sphere of the Gospel, our children have value and worth both in God's eyes and in their parents' eyes; therefore, they should see themselves as valuable also.

4. *Our children have worth because of who they are (or can become in Christ).* Jesus Himself said in Matthew 16:25, "For whoever wishes to save his life shall lose it; but whoever loses his life for My sake shall find it." When, by God's grace, our children are enabled to forsake self and yield their allegiance to Jesus Christ, they will know their true identity. They will never be totally satisfied with themselves until they find forgiveness and ongoing cleansing in Him. In Him, they will become new creations (2 Cor. 5:17). And through His strength they will become equipped to do all things (Phil. 4:13). Jesus Christ will have become to them "wisdom from God, and righteousness and sanctification, and redemption" (1 Cor. 1:30). In Christ they will have value par excellence.

Because there are so many solid reasons for children of believers to have a healthy self-regard, it is most unfortunate that, as Strommen says:

> Analysis shows that one out of four [teens] is much troubled by thoughts of personal blame. An additional one in two admits to being somewhat bothered by these feelings. This is an affliction known in varying degrees, by most youth. . . . More than three out of five (62 percent) of those *most* troubled by feelings of low self-esteem admit to thoughts of self-destruction.[3]

My own research leads me to concur with Strommen's findings. I recognize that a degree of self-criticism is good and natural for maturing young people. But when a quarter of them are so down on themselves that their poor self-esteem interferes with relationships and creates feelings of anxiety and worthlessness, there is cause for alarm.

The way our children perceive themselves begins with the way they think about themselves. Perceptions that are maintained over a long period of time will harden into convictions, and convictions formed by negative criticism, harsh words, and the absence of positive expressions of love and acceptance, will lead to feelings of worthlessness. Strommen identifies three characteristics, in particular, that identify a child who has a problem in this area: (1) distress over personal faults, (2) lack of self-confidence, (3) low self-regard.

NURTURE YOUR CHILD'S SELF-ESTEEM

In their early years, our children's view of themselves is shaped almost entirely by what we, as their parents, convey to them through our words and actions. Even in their adolescent and teen years, when their peers begin to exert a greater influence on their self-perception, our children still remain sensitive to what Mom and Dad think about them. If we desire to help them develop a healthy self-esteem, we must communicate to them those things that will help them perceive themselves as God does. For most of us, this will necessitate a constant reexamining of both what we are saying to our children and how we are saying it. Often, the *manner* in which we speak to them is more harmful than the actual *content* of our words. Even the tone of our voice can betray a negative *attitude* to our children so that the content of our words means very little to them. For instance, if you consistently speak to your children in a sullen, abrupt, or demanding way, they may assume that you are displeased with them even when, in reality, you are not. If you fail to show a positive, enthusiastic response every time they bring home an acceptable report card, they may conclude that you are displeased with their efforts even though you said nothing negative about their grades.

One of the hallmarks of evangelical theology is its emphasis on the sinful nature of man. This is as it should be. But unless our children are also hearing about God's prescribed remedy for their sin, they are likely to develop a sense of total worthlessness. Nothing can be more harmful to one's feelings of self-esteem than being regularly wounded by God's law without, at the same time, experiencing the healing balm of God's love and grace in Christ. As Christian parents, then, we must be careful to deal with our children's sin by always pointing them to Jesus Christ as the One who can give them victory over sin (Rom. 7:24-25).

Apart from the question of how to confront our children regarding their sin, how can we best develop in them a healthy self-esteem—one that will give them a feeling of belonging, of being worthwhile and capable individuals with potential for growth? I suggest that the most important area of concern ought to be the manner in which we speak to our children. Solomon of old placed great emphasis on the power of the tongue. In Proverbs 18:21 he said, "Death and life are in the power of the tongue." James, likewise, compares the tongue to a fountain that can bring forth bitter or sweet water, curses or blessings (James 3:8-12). In other words, Scripture reminds us that the words we speak to our children can be a blessing to them, or they can lead to their emotional and spiritual destruction.

We read in Proverbs 15:2: "The tongue of the wise makes knowledge acceptable." And Proverbs 16:21 tells us: "Sweetness of speech increases persuasiveness [lit. learning]." Our words, or the manner in which we say them, may not be able to manufacture faith in the hearts of our children, but the promise of these verses is that a wise and pleasant tongue will make our children more open to accepting the truth. Pleasant speech will, at the very least, create a climate in which they will listen to God's Word and be more apt to believe it.

AVOID ROTTEN WORDS

What is this "sweet speech" that Solomon mentions in Proverbs 16:21? I suggest to you that it is the kind of talk

Paul refers to in Colossians 4:6 when he says, "Let your speech always be with grace, seasoned, as it were, with salt, so that you may know how you should respond to each person." This "sweet speech," however, is most clearly defined in Ephesians 4:29:

> Let no unwholesome word proceed from your mouth, but only such a word as is good for edification according to the need of the moment, that it may give grace to those who hear.

In the context, Paul is reminding the believers at Ephesus that they should behave as those who are putting off the old self and putting on the new self (v. 24). Although he is referring to how the Christian should live before all men in general and fellow believers in particular, Paul's directives may also properly be applied to the way parents live before their children. It is with this narrower interpretation that we will examine Ephesians 4:29.

The verse divides into two sections—a negative command and a positive one. He says first, "Don't allow any unwholesome word to proceed from your mouth." The word *unwholesome* is a word used to describe rotten trees or rotten fruit. When applied to rotten words, *unwholesome* can have a very broad application, referring to words that are profane, vulgar, obscene, unkind, or dishonest. Whatever these unwholesome words may be, they all have one thing in common: they have the stench of death about them. They hurt the one to whom they are directed. As James 3:8 explains, "[The tongue] is a restless evil and full of deadly poison."

I'm sure the last thing you want to do as a parent is to wound your children with words full of deadly poison. And yet, the sad fact is that even in Christian homes, unwholesome, rotten, poisonous barbs flow from the lips of well-meaning parents. If such talk is characteristic of the way parents speak to their children, the following results are likely to occur: first, the children's sense of self-esteem will be severely distorted; second, the children will lose all respect for the parents; and finally, the children will have little interest in seriously considering the parents' faith.

Fritz Ridenour, in his helpful book, *What Teenagers Wish Their Parents Knew about Kids,* lists several kinds of unwholesome or deadly words.[4] He calls them, "communication killers." I suggest they could also be called "faith-formation killers" because they destroy first our children's sense of self-worth and then their interest in their parents' faith. Following are some types of words that Ridenour believes destroy our children.

1. *Gunslinger Words.* These are words that tend to blow our kids away with one shot:

● "So you're wearing that ugly outfit again?"

● "I don't think you'll ever be smart enough to get an *A.*"

● "There you go, acting like a real idiot again."

These are words we fire at our children, especially at our adolescents, when we are trying to be cutting, sarcastic, or cynical. No matter what the motive, they are hurtful words and, as Ridenour puts it, "He who lives by Gunslinger Words sees communication die by same."[5]

2. *Defensive Words.* When our children speak to us in a sarcastic or irritating manner, we may be tempted to return evil for evil. I'm not suggesting we ignore their rudeness, but if we have encouraged our children to speak what's on their mind, we must not expect that everything they say will be sweet and edifying.

No matter how hard we try, there are going to be times when everything within us reacts defensively: "Who do you think you are talking to me that way? You had better get your own act together. And furthermore...."

In the previous chapter we looked at James 1:19 which

reminds us that we are to be quick to hear but slow to speak and slow to anger. If ever we should follow this counsel, it is on those occasions when we are tempted to strike back at our children with defensive words. It is then that "the heart of the righteous [parent] ponders how to answer" (Prov. 15:28).

3. *Discouraging Words.* These are generally put-down words or critical words that destroy our children's sense of self-esteem. They are words that will "exasperate your children" so that they "lose heart" (Col. 3:21). Often, discouraging words will come forth as absolute statements like:

● "You are *always* disobedient."

● "I can *never* trust you to do what you promise."

● "Not a *single day* goes by that you don't go against my word!"

Speaking in absolutes is probably one of the biggest put-downs and destroyers of self-esteem that we parents practice. We must remember that absolute statements usually aren't true. Secondly, they communicate to our children that even when they say or do the right thing, we don't notice. So why should they bother trying?

Another kind of discouraging word insists on immediate obedience with no thought whatsoever to the need or situation of the child. For example, you ask your son to take out the garbage. He says, "I'm right in the middle of a difficult math problem, Mom. Can I finish it first and then take out the garbage?"

You respond, "No, you can't! Get down here immediately and do what I tell you to do when I tell you."

In a situation like this what you are saying to your son is: "I don't really care about your schedule. I have no respect for your wishes, only for my own." You are most assuredly creating in your son a feeling of total helplessness and resentment. Your words will cause him to conclude: "Even when I talk nice to Mom, I get yelled at. I can't ever win with her."

4. *Double Meaning Words.* These words carry a double message that leaves the child confused about what we are *really* saying:

- "Oh, we'll see. . . ."

- "Maybe you can go."

- "Maybe later. . . ."

Usually we say these kinds of things when we are too lazy to think through our children's request or when we are too afraid of a confrontation if we don't give them the response they want to hear. In any case, by putting them off, we are again communicating to them that their request is not that important to us. We ought to tell them the truth in love, and that means avoiding any double-meaning words (Eph. 4:15).

5. *Nagging Words.* Ridenour records the response of one fourteen-year-old who described his parents as "Don't, Don't, Don't, No! No! No! Stop! Stop! Stop! NAG! NAG! NAG!"[6] Parents certainly do have a right to remind their children of what they have already been asked to do; however, what we tend to view as reminders, our children often interpret as nagging. They usually come to that conclusion not so much because of our further reminder but because of the sermon we attach to the reminder or the impatient tone of our voice. If at all possible, reminders should be given in a warm, hang-loose manner. We should state our case clearly and briefly and seek some sort of response from our children. As they get older, they can even be given freedom to negotiate with us on how and when the assignment is to be done. This will show them that we respect both their opinion and their schedule.

Nagging words are some of the most common unwholesome or destructive words that parents use in communicating with their children. They tend to destroy our children's sense of self-worth, break down the parent-child relationship, and ultimately harden them against seriously considering the Christian faith.

6. *Silent Words.* One additional negative way of communicating with our children is by giving them the silent treatment. We display our displeasure with them by saying nothing at all. Even when they ask us questions, we speak no words but instead grunt or look away in disgust. This is not only rude, but it is very frustrating for the children. There may be times when, because of our anger, we must delay our response (James 1:19), but to give no answer at all is to place a further barrier to good communication.

SPEAK WORDS THAT BUILD UP
In Ephesians 4:29, we are reminded of the types of words we *should* use with our children.

1. *Our words should be "good for edification according to the need."*

As parents we must ask ourselves the question: Are our words meeting an immediate need? Often parents get carried away in their response to their children and end up lecturing them on something other than the subject at hand. I suppose we feel that since we already have their attention, we might as well get in as many licks as possible: "And while we are on the subject of clothes, young man, your closet is an absolute mess. Your underwear is never in the wash, and I really think you should be wearing more deodorant."

All the poor boy asked his mom was, "Should I wear this orange shirt with my purple pants?" But he got a three-point sermon on something else.

Paul's advice to this mother, and to many of us, is that we speak only to the need at hand. As Solomon says in Proverbs 15:23, "A man has joy in an apt answer, and how delightful is a timely word." What this means is that we must first learn—as we said in the last chapter—to stop, look, and listen before we begin to speak. We must ask ourselves, "What is my child really saying? Does he want my opinion on his choice of clothes, or is he after my approval of him as a person?" We must take the time to speak words that are appropriate according to the need.

2. *Our words should be "good for edification."*

We must ask ourselves the question: Are our words going to build up our children? The word *edification* means to build up, to strengthen, to make strong. In other words, when we speak to our children, our goal must always be to strengthen them. Paul is thinking primarily of being strengthened in the spiritual dimension but, as we've seen before, it is impossible to separate our children's emotional well-being from their spiritual well-being. If our words build up their sense of self-esteem, our children will be more likely to give ear to spiritual things.

So instead of telling your son that his color coordination is the worst you've ever seen or that you suspect he's trying to imitate his friends at school, you could say, "Bobby, those sure are brilliant colors. The styles go together well, but maybe a more neutral-colored shirt would blend better."

You may still have an argument on your hands, but most likely you won't. Better still, by building him up instead of tearing him down, you have not discredited your son's abilities; you have aided him to think through his decision a little more carefully. This may seem like a very minor incident, but most of our confrontations begin over minor incidents.

3. *Our words should "give grace to those who hear."*

We must ask ourselves: Are our words ministering grace to our children? This means our words should be spiritually beneficial to our children by somehow promoting God's work of grace in their lives. In Proverbs 12:18 we read, "There is one who speaks rashly like the thrusts of a sword

[destructive words], but the tongue of the wise brings healing." The tongue of the wise parent ministers grace and
spiritual strength to his children. His speech is always with
grace (Col. 4:6). It is said of Jesus in Luke 4:22 that, "All
were speaking well of Him, and wondering at the gracious
words which were falling from His lips." Gracious words,
edifying words, words needful for the moment just fell
from our Lord's mouth. We, on the other hand, have to
work hard to be able to speak such words.

The implication of Paul's statement in Ephesians 4:29 is
that if we speak to our children with words that are needful and edifying, these words will also tend to minister
grace to them. God will use our tongues as instruments of
healing and fountains of life, not just to promote in our
children a sense of self-worth but, more importantly, to
lead them to an enduring faith in Jesus Christ.

For Review, Discussion, and Action:

1. What four foundational reasons does Christianity give
for believing our children have great worth?

2. Discuss a biblical view of self-esteem in our children by
examining the following Scriptures: Matthew 10:39; 16:24-
25; 22:34-40; ; 1 Corinthians 1:30; Philippians 4:13; 1 John 3:1

3. Discuss and illustrate from your own life the following
kinds of words that we should avoid using with our children: gunslinger words, defensive words, discouraging
words, double-meaning words, nagging words, and silent
words.

4. Which of the kinds of words mentioned in question 3 are
characteristic of the way you talk to your children? What
do you plan to do in order to change?

5. Based on Ephesians 4:29, discuss the three qualities our

words should have in order to be truly beneficial to our children. Think of specific ways you exemplify these qualities.

6. If you have used destructive words with your children and never asked them to forgive you, go to your children today and make things right. Ask them to help you in the future by telling you when the things you say hurt or anger them.

For Further Study:

Adams, Jay E. *The Biblical View of Self-Esteem, Self-Love and Self-Image.* Eugene: Harvest House Publishers, 1986. In my opinion this is the most biblical work thus far on the question of self-image and self-esteem.

Mack, Wayne. *A Homework Manual for Biblical Counselors.* Vol. 1. Phillipsburg: Presbyterian and Reformed Publishing Company, 1979. On pages 177–178, Dr. Mack challenges the reader to develop a personal view of self-love by examining the pertinent biblical verses.

Mack, Wayne. *A Homework Manual for Biblical Counselors.* Vol. 2. Phillipsburg: Presbyterian and Reformed Publishing Company, 1980. The author provides helpful guidelines for communication on pages 10–12. On page 13, Dr. Mack provides a list of numerous biblical verses dealing with how we should speak and should not speak.

Ridenour, Fritz. *What Teenagers Wish Their Parents Knew about Kids.* Waco: Word Books, 1982. The "Communication Killers" already referred to in our text are discussed at length in chapter 5, "Communication Needs Tender Loving Care."

Strommen, Merton P. *Five Cries of Youth.* San Francisco:

Harper & Row Publishers, 1974. In chapter 2, Strommen deals with the subject of self-hatred among youth. He covers both its causes and potential cures.

CHAPTER NINE

COMMUNICATE A MESSAGE OF TRUST

Faith-formation Principle: *To help our children come to an enduring faith in Christ, we must demonstrate the essence of that faith, not only by our trust in God, but also by our willingness to trust our children.*

Biblical Text: 1 Corinthians 13:7

I had turned sixteen on Monday. Two days later I passed my driver's test and received my long-awaited operator's license. On Friday night of the same week, my father allowed me to take his beautiful, aqua-green, 1956 Monarch away for the weekend. Three other teenagers and I were attending an Inter-School Christian Fellowship retreat some eighty miles from home.

Not too many fathers would entrust their sixteen-year-old sons with that kind of responsibility. But my father was a very trusting man. Granted, I had come a long way in my driving ability since the tractor hitch fiasco six years earlier (see chapter 6), but I still had only a few months of driver's training under my belt. I suppose, at the time, I simply assumed it was quite natural for my parents to trust me. They always had. Although I did not really appreciate it

at the time, I have come to recognize over the years that
the confidence my parents placed in me as I was growing
up was one of many factors that contributed to my openness to the Christian faith. Their trust in me not only increased my love for them and my desire to please them
and be worthy of their trust, but it also provided me with a
visible model of what is involved in true faith.

MODEL TRUE FAITH

Most Christian parents would be quick to agree that they
should exemplify a life of trust in God—trust for salvation
and trust for daily needs. We know that our children can
learn how to trust God by observing our own pattern of
faith in Him. Hebrews 11 reminds us that the faith of previous generations is to serve as a model and an encouragement for succeeding ones.

The character of true faith can also be modeled by the
way we express trust in our own children as they are growing up in our home. Think for a moment of the basic qualities of biblical faith.

1. *True faith involves believing in the promises of
God's Word.* Solomon, at the dedication of the temple
prays, "Blessed be the Lord, who has given rest to His
people Israel, according to all that He promised; not one
word has failed of all His good promise" (1 Kings 8:56). The
conviction that God is always true to His own Word is the
foundation of biblical faith. If the Apostle Paul had not
truly believed that God's Word was trustworthy, he could
never have told his fellow passengers as they were about
to be shipwrecked, "Keep up your courage, men, for I believe God, that it will turn out exactly as I have been told"
(Acts 27:25).

In a similar way, when our children promise something,
and we take them at their word, we are exercising faith in
them. We are saying, in essence, "I believe you that it will
turn out exactly as I have been told."

2. *True faith expresses confidence in God's abilities.*

Not only do we trust in the veracity of His Word, but we also trust in the capability of His person. We believe He *can* do what He *said* He would do. In particular, when we exercise faith in Him, we rest in His qualities of faithfulness (1 Cor. 10:13; 2 Thes. 3:3; Heb. 10:23; 1 John 1:9) and power (Gen. 18:14; Dan. 3:17; Matt. 19:26).

When I say we should trust our children, I am not suggesting we should place confidence in them beyond what they are intellectually, emotionally, or physically capable of doing. My father did not trust me with the family car when I was ten years old because I had not yet sufficiently demonstrated the maturity or skill necessary to warrant that trust. Six years later, however, I did show that I was capable of such a responsibility. Parents must know their children well enough to determine what kinds of responsibilities they can handle at each stage of their growth. If parents burden children with responsibilities greater than they can handle, the whole process of trust-building could backfire. A child could become discouraged, guilt-ridden, or resentful. And repeated failure to complete difficult responsibilities could leave the parents with the conviction that their son or daughter is not trustworthy. How important it is, therefore, that we understand our children's individual strengths and weaknesses and look for opportunities to entrust them with responsibilities and privileges they can master.

3. *True faith anticipates accountability.* God makes Himself accountable to His Word by tying His promises to His very nature as One who cannot lie (Num. 23:19; Heb. 6:13-18). He cannot go back on His Word without denying His very existence (2 Tim. 2:13). Our knowledge that He is not afraid to be called into account for His actions tends to increase our faith in His promises to us.

When we trust our children, we must always make it clear that we hold them responsible for their actions. There can be no privilege or responsibility without an accompanying accountability. As we shall see later, it is this very

sense of accountability to parents that a child must ultimately transfer to the Lord. Accountability must be present
for true faith to flourish.

True faith, then, the kind of faith we desire to see our
children ultimately place in Jesus Christ for salvation, can
be modeled—though ever so imperfectly—by the way we
as parents express our confidence in our children. In earlier childhood they may only intuitively sense that Mommy
and Daddy trust them. But as they progress through their
adolescent and teenage years and begin to do more analyti-
cal and reflective thinking about life, they will tend to appreciate more fully the significance of our expressions of
faith in them. Furthermore, as God is pleased to accompany this modeling of true faith with His saving influences,
we can anticipate that most children will find it quite natural to put their faith in Christ for salvation.

In 1 Corinthians 13:7-8, the Apostle Paul defines true love
by saying, "Love... bears all things, believes all things,
hopes all things, endures all things. Love never fails." The
NIV states, "Love... always trusts." Parents who want to
act in love toward their children must learn to trust them.
That kind of love, says Paul, "never fails."

The question is, how do we go about trusting our children "always" or "in all things"? Does this mean we believe
them even when we know they are lying? Obviously not.
Paul is not commanding us to ignore all the evidence and
believe our children at any cost. But when there is no
evidence available, and we are left with only the word of
the child, loving parents trust. They say, "OK. Since only
God can see your heart, I take you at your word and hold
you accountable to it."

Apart from those times when parents must decide
whether or not to believe a child's story or excuse, how
may we as parents consistently demonstrate our love for
our children through the act of trusting them? Of course
we can do this in a number of different ways, but I would
like to flesh out just two of them.

BE A DEPARENTING PARENT

One way to define the goal of parenting is to describe it as "parenting to deparent." By deparenting I mean the art of training our children to assume increasing responsibility for their own total welfare so as to be set free from dependency on their parents.[1] To deparent does not mean becoming a nonparent. It does mean giving up more and more control over the lives of our children and becoming more their guide, their encourager, and their friend.

The Lord Himself was the first to imply the need for a deparenting process when He said in Genesis 2:24, "For this cause a man shall leave his father and his mother, and shall cleave to his wife; and they shall become one flesh." The implied assumption of the text is not only that the father and mother are willing to let their sons and daughters go, but also that the parents have prepared their offspring to assume their new responsibilities as man and wife. This is what I call the deparenting process. It begins at birth and continues until the child leaves home as a fully functioning adult.

When that cuddly bundle of love first enters your home, your little one is totally dependent on you for everything. But as the child develops physiologically and improves his motor, mental, and verbal skills, you can begin the deparenting process. It basically involves two steps: (1) the giving of responsibilities and (2) the giving of freedoms or privileges.

I am especially eager to stress that the act of deparenting demands a willingness to trust your children. You must trust them to fulfill the responsibilities you give them. You must trust them not to abuse the freedoms or privileges you grant them. Your children will have to be trusted more and more in both of these areas if they are to be prepared to leave mother and father and begin a family of their own. What starts out as totally the parent's domain of responsibility becomes in time, through the deparenting process, totally the child's domain of responsibility. And the time to start trusting them is when they are very young.

For example, take the fine art of toilet training. Sooner or later you must hold the child responsible for exercise of self-control in this matter. But you must also be willing to trust him: "If Mommy doesn't put a diaper on you today, will you tell her when you have to go to the potty?"

"Uh huh!"

"Uh huh" may not be much of a promise, but it's all you are going to get at this point, and you must trust your child to keep it. If he consistently fails to tell you when he needs to use the bathroom, you may have to withdraw, temporarily, the privilege of freedom from diapers. At this age, verbal explanation alone is not sufficient; your child must also experience the physical loss of privilege in order to understand the relationship between freedom and responsibility.

As children grow older, more and more areas of responsibility must be entrusted to them. This will involve negotiating with your children so that they have more input about the responsibilities and freedoms you give them. For instance, when your daughter is a preschooler, you must choose what she wears. But there comes a point when you must allow her, under your instruction, to make her own choices. Ultimately, of course, she must take full responsibility for this matter.

Even as I was writing the above paragraph, my twelve-year-old, Lynn, came into my room and said, "Dad, I need some new clothes for school. Do you think Laura (her eighteen-year-old sister) could take me to the mall this Friday so I could buy something?"

What do I say, "No! Your mother must go with you"? Or do I give her some money and say, "All right, I trust you to exercise wisdom in what you purchase with this money"? I chose the latter course, and she was very happy.

At each stage of this deparenting process, we are called on to place more and more trust in our children's abilities to make wise choices. With each additional responsibility successfully assumed and with each additional privilege successfully honored, our children build capital for further responsibilities and freedoms. At the same time, we are building capital in our "trust bank," on which we can draw for future occasions when we will have to entrust our children with even greater responsibilities and freedoms.

Perhaps by now some of you are wondering what to do when your child violates your trust. Let's assume you have just given your son a task to do which you believe is fair and reasonable. He promises to do it. But then he fails to follow through. What should you do? Some parents would say, "Immediately withdraw the freedoms or privileges attached to the responsibility you gave your son." I agree that at times you will have to do this as a form of equitable discipline; however, you must remember that you are trying to communicate to your child a spirit of trust.

We must realize that our children will fail from time to time. We all fail ourselves. What happens to us when we do not faithfully fulfill our marital or parental responsibilities, or when we violate the freedoms God has given us as the leaders in the family? Does our Heavenly Father take away our privileges and responsibilities as husbands and wives and parents? Of course not! So then, let us not be too quick to "ground" our children when they abuse a privilege or fail to carry out a responsibility we have given them. It could be that our willingness to trust them, even when they fail, will be the most convincing expression of confidence we could ever give them. There is no better place for our children to fail than in the loving, accepting environment of their own home.

Consider the following principles for communicating a spirit of trust to our children:

1. *We should discuss with our children the possible consequence for violating our trust.* The older they are, the more input we should give our children regarding both details of assigned tasks and the consequences of not fulfilling their responsibilities. Contrary to public opinion, they may be harder on themselves than we would be. We

must be sure that they clearly understand both the nature of their responsibilities and/or privileges and the consequences of failing to honor them. Armed with such an understanding, our children will have difficulty accusing us later of being unfair or of not trusting them when they fail.

2. *We must be willing to allow our children to learn from their failures.* The natural tendency of loving parents is to protect their children from unnecessary pain or disappointment. On many occasions, however, the most loving thing we can do is allow our children to suffer the natural consequences of their actions.

For example, if your son constantly forgets to take his lunch to school, instead of delivering it to him personally, perhaps the best thing you could do would be to allow him to go without lunch a few times. If your daughter consistently fails to practice her violin and then wants you to cancel her next lesson, perhaps you should allow her to suffer the embarrassment of going to a lesson unprepared rather than giving into her pleas.

Children need to learn that they must live with the consequences of their decisions. If we always bail them out of their self-inflicted problems, we will be removing a natural context for personal growth. Indeed, our overparenting may actually retard the deparenting process. If the Lord allows His children to reap what they have sown (Gal. 6:7-9) in order that they might ultimately bring forth the "fruit of righteousness" (Heb. 12:11), surely we ought be willing to do the same with our children.

3. *Ultimately, we want our children to transfer their sense of accountability from us to God.* Small children generally have no problem realizing that they are accountable to their parents; however, they must be taught that one day they will also give an account to God for everything they do (Rom. 14:12). The more responsibilities and privileges we place into their hands, the more accountable they become to the Lord. In Luke 12:48 Jesus says, "And from everyone who has been given much shall much be

required: and to whom they entrusted much, of him they will ask all the more." Our children need to realize that being raised within the sphere of Gospel influence by parents who trust them brings them into an accountability with God Himself.

Our children may think they can put one over on Mom and Dad, but when they have been taught that "each one of us shall give an account of himself to God," they will be less likely to shirk their responsibilities or abuse their privileges. Happy, then, are the children who learn how to be accountable to their parents. They will have a much easier time placing themselves under the all-seeing eyes of the Heavenly Father than will children who have not learned to be accountable to anyone.

When our children violate the trust we have placed in them, we should always keep these three principles in mind. We must take the time to ask ourselves important questions:

1. Have we made clear to our children the possible consequences of violating our trust?

2. How can we best respond to their failure so that they will learn the lessons of faith God wants to teach them?

3. What can we do in the situation to underscore their ultimate accountability to God?

These are the questions that ought to guide our decisions as we seek to be faithful in the deparenting process.

BE A TRANSPARENT PARENT

According to young people who participated in the Youth Congress '85 questionnaire, hypocrisy in adults was one reason for forsaking the faith. This hypocrisy, in part, is conveyed by our unwillingness, especially as parents, to be open with our children regarding our own weaknesses, failures, and sins. I have already touched on this subject but, because it has a direct relationship to what we are considering in this present chapter, I want to remind you of it once more.

Most of us want to be models of the faith that will attract our children to confess allegiance to Jesus Christ. Somewhere along the line, we have concluded that the more perfect we appear in their eyes, the more impressed they will be with our model and the more attracted they will be to Christianity.

I am convinced that nothing could be further from the truth. Not only does this kind of thinking depend on incorrect analysis of how to model the faith, but it is also deceptive and dangerous. It is deceptive because no one can live the Christian life perfectly; it is dangerous because instead of attracting our children to consider Christ, it drives them away. One of the common complaints I heard from people who had rejected the faith was: "My parents acted as if they could do no wrong. They always had the right answers at the right time. When there was tension in the family, it was always caused by someone else, not by them. After awhile I started to think that Christianity was only for perfect people, and that left me out."

How tragic! What our children need to see in the home is not perfect parents but forgiven sinners who are faithfully striving to overcome remaining sins by applying the principles of God's Word. It is not the vision of a sinless saint that will attract our children to Christ, but it is the opportunity to live with parents who are willing to make themselves vulnerable to their children by being open and honest with them.

The main point of being transparent parents is that we are again showing our children we trust them. For example, if we know we have sinned against one of our children and we go and ask forgiveness, we are trusting that child to grant us forgiveness. When we admit to our faults or acknowledge that we don't have answers to all the problems confronting us, we are trusting them not to lose respect for us. Some parents aren't willing to risk their parental image by being that transparent with their children. But, in the long haul, they will be the very parents who will lose the respect and admiration of their children.

The truth of the matter is, we can fool our children only so long, and then they will see through our mask. When they are younger, they may not understand that we are trying to hide our own sins and weaknesses, but they will begin to develop a certain attitude of distrust in us. And worse than that, if we persist in playing the hypocrite, they will probably transfer that attitude of distrust to God also.

If you are one of those parents who still insists, "My children must *earn* my trust before I will give them freedoms and responsibilities and before I will ever make myself vulnerable to them," then you are probably going to lose your children. How can they demonstrate they are worthy of your trust unless they are given freedoms and responsibilities for which you can hold them accountable?

I am so thankful that God did not come to me and say: "Carl, I really love you. I want the best for you in this life. I really do. But, you are going to have to prove to Me first that you are trustworthy. I am going to have to be convinced that you can keep My laws perfectly before I give you the full privileges and freedoms of sonship in My family." If God had taken that approach with me, I would still be lost in my sin.

But, praise His name, He did not demand I prove myself first. Instead, He loved me by giving me all the privileges and freedoms and blessings of sonship simply because I'm His child. Oh, He's had plenty of disciplining to do along the way, and I'm sure I will give Him cause for more in the future, but His love led Him to trust me with His salvation even when He knew I would fail. In a sense, He was transparent with me, and made Himself vulnerable to the disappointments and the hurts I would inflict upon Him by my sin and disobedience. Yet, He has continued to entrust Himself to me.

If we really love our children and desire to see them

come to an abiding faith in Christ, then we too must learn to communicate to them an attitude of trust by being deparenting parents and transparent parents.

For Review, Discussion, and Action:

1. Reread the faith-formation principle at the beginning of this chapter. Now write your own amplified version of the same principle.

2. What three characteristics of our faith in God are especially important for us to model by the kind of trust we place in our children?

3. Discuss the meaning of 1 Corinthians 13:7: "Love . . . believes all things." Give several examples of situations in your relationship with your children in which it is especially difficult for you to fulfill this command.

4. List five specific things you are doing now as part of the process of deparenting. In what ways are you keeping your children dependent on you? Why are you doing it?

5. What specific things are you doing to help your children transfer their sense of accountability from you to God?

6. In what ways are you being a transparent parent? How are you putting on a mask with your children? What are you afraid will happen if you make yourself vulnerable to your children?

7. Why shouldn't we expect our children to earn our trust first?

For Further Study:

Herring, Reuben and Dorothy. *Becoming Friends with*

Your Children. Nashville: Broadman Press, 1984. In chapters 5 and 6 the Herrings deal with numerous matters related to the final stage of the deparenting process—letting your children go to establish a home of their own.

Ridenour, Fritz. *What Teenagers Wish Their Parents Knew about Kids.* Waco: Word Books, 1982. In chapter 3 Ridenour deals with the issue of deparenting and how to let go of our children.

Stanley, Charles. *How to Keep Your Kids on Your Team.* Nashville: Oliver Nelson Publishers, 1986. Dr. Stanley offers some helpful counsel in chapter 9 on how parents can transfer the control and responsibility of their children over to God.

CHAPTER TEN

PROVOKE NOT TO WRATH

Faith-formation Principle: *In order to help our children come to an enduring faith in Christ, we must not provoke them to wrath but bring them up in the discipline and admonition of the Lord.*

Biblical Texts: Ephesians 6:4; Colossians 3:21

Those of you who are familiar with the biblical passages related to parenting suspected, I'm sure, that sooner or later we would be dealing with Ephesians 6:4 and Colossians 3:21. You were absolutely correct. These verses contain few words, but the message those words convey is of inestimable value for parents who desire to lead their children to an enduring faith in Jesus Christ.

In personal interviews with those who have forsaken the faith, I discovered that very often these people rejected the faith because of anger against parents and an accompanying feeling of never being able to please parents. Both of these emotions (anger and hopelessness) were often related to the parents' failure to fulfill the positive aspect of Paul's instruction: bring up children in the discipline and admonition of the Lord.

Obviously, the apostle knew what parents had to do in order to keep their kids in the faith. The question is, "Are we really willing to follow his counsel?" Most of us probably know Ephesians 6:4 and Colossians 3:21 by memory. Unfortunately, our mental awareness of what God's Word says about parenting is not enough; these principles must also be implemented as a natural and ongoing part of the parenting process. It is with that goal in mind that we will thoroughly exam the instruction provided for us in these two verses.

FATHERS, BE WARNED

Notice the emphasis in each verse on the role of the father:

"Fathers, do not provoke your children to anger" (Eph. 6:4).

"Fathers, do not exasperate your children" (Col. 3:21).

Certainly the warning stands for mothers as well as for fathers. But because Paul does not use the standard word for parents here as he had in the verses preceding these texts, his specific choice of the word *father* seems deliberate (Eph. 6:1; Col. 3:20). He desires to focus attention on the fathers in particular. This should not surprise us because God has given fathers ultimate responsibility for the training of their children. In Paul's day, fathers were given freedom to treat their children in almost any way they desired. Consider the following quotation:

A Roman father had absolute power over his family. He could sell them as slaves, he could make them work in his fields even in chains, he could take the law into his own hands and punish as he liked, he could even inflict the death penalty on his children.[1]

In a society like that, the Christian father who faithfully followed Paul's directives on training children would have stood out like a sore thumb. If he showed any expression of love to his children, especially to his sons, he might have been considered weak and effeminate by his Roman neighbors. Yet, the Christian faith demanded radical changes in every area of social life, including the marital and parental areas. It still does today. And, fathers, we must be the primary agents in helping our families follow the Lord's standards, not those of the world. This means that we must heed Paul's wise warnings not to provoke our children to anger.

DON'T PROVOKE
In Ephesians 6:4 Paul uses a word that means, "to be angry with resentment." It is the same word found in Ephesians 4:26, where he says we should not allow the sun to go down on our anger. In other words, just as we should not go to bed provoked or embittered against our children, we should never give them cause to go to bed feeling that way toward us. We must not provoke them or give them a reason to become resentful or embittered against us.

We should not, of course, become so paranoid over the possibility of angering our children that we never correct them or discipline them or do anything that might make them angry with us. Our children will get angry with us from time to time, just as we will get angry with them. But when we habitually and unnecessarily provoke them to become angry with us, or when we regularly allow them to go to bed with feelings of resentment against us, we are developing angry young men and women. That, I believe, is what Paul warns us against.

In Colossians 3:21 Paul adds another dimension that gives us a better idea of the kind of situation he is envisioning. He says, "Fathers, do not exasperate your children, that they may not lose heart." The expression "to lose heart" conveys the idea of becoming discouraged or spiritless in the extreme. One author says, "so that the wind is taken out of their sails."

The sad fact is that many fathers (parents) have been guilty of doing this to their children. They have angered them so much for so long that their children have just given up trying to please them. Under these circumstances, young people are very unlikely to be open to the Christian faith as professed by their parents. I spoke with one teenager who told me she could hardly wait to get out of her home: "Everything I ever do is not good enough for my parents, especially my father. I feel like I have to always be on my guard about what I say and do. I'm getting to the point where I feel hatred for him—yet I love him." I wasn't surprised that this girl was already pregnant out of wedlock and thinking about marrying her boyfriend. She would do anything to get away from the oppressive atmosphere at home.

Children who have been provoked to wrath over a long period of time usually express their anger in two basic ways.

1. *Some angry children seethe inwardly.* This will often be the response of children who are not allowed to speak freely in the home. Because they have not been told how to talk through their feelings of anger with their parents, they bottle them up. Their anger may become so all-consuming that it influences everything they do. As Paul says in Colossians 3:21, they "lose heart." They become apathetic about their studies, their social life, and their own appearance. They begin to withdraw and may ultimately commit suicide or act out their anger through violent criminal acts such as rape and murder.

2. *Some angry children explode outwardly.* Most children do this at one time or another. (With young children we call this kind of behavior a temper tantrum.) The problem arises when parents provoke their sons and daughters to wrath over a long period of time. These young people develop the habit of expressing their rebellious spirit by blowing up. Eventually, they begin exploding not only at the unjust provocations of their parents but also at the slightest provocations by anyone. They become "hot tempered" people (Prov. 14:29; 15:18; 29:11).

BE AWARE OF
PROBABLE CAUSES OF PROVOCATION

So what do we as parents do that provokes our children to anger? The following list contains some probable causes. I use the word *probable* because, depending on the presence or absence of other factors in the parent-child relationship, these actions may not always cause our children to become angry with us. However, experience dictates that in most cases these actions can lead to the kind of resentful and hopeless feelings that Paul talks about in our texts.

1. *We provoke our children with destructive criticism.* I have already alluded to this kind of parental action in chapter 8 when we considered the kinds of words we should speak to our children. Peter, referring to Proverbs 10:12, says, "Above all, keep fervent in your love for one another, because love covers a multitude of sins (1 Peter 4:8). In other words, if we love our children, we will not point out to them their every mistake or irritating action. We especially will not rebuke them for purely childish behavior that is expected of children their age. For example, if your five-year-old fails to keep within the lines of the picture he is coloring for you, or accidently trips over a toy on the floor and spills the glass of water he was bringing you, you should not accuse him of being sloppy or careless.

Some children cannot sneeze without their parents telling them they didn't do it correctly. One of our daughters tends to "wake the dead" whenever she blows her nose, an action that irritates me considerably, probably because she learned how to do it by listening to her father blow his nose. It is a real struggle for me not to constantly rebuke her for being so loud and unladylike in this particular matter. In the long run, the small matter of the way she blows her nose should not be made a cause of tension between us.

When all our children hear from morning to night is criticism of what they are doing or not doing, they will become totally disheartened before long. And they will probably develop a very negative self-image and/or openly rebel against their parents and their parents' faith.

One of the skills most of us parents have not learned is the fine art of encouragement through praise. If we spent more time praising our children for the things they did right, or even attempted to do right, they would give us less cause to be critical of them. Solomon says it best: "There is one who speaks rashly like the thrusts of a sword, but the tongue of the wise brings healing" (Prov. 12:18).

2. *We provoke our children by abusing them physically or emotionally.* We are living in an age teeming with the destructive consequences of physical child abuse. Christian parents must not think they are immune to the possibility of abusing their own children. The Bible does encourage corporal punishment through the use of the rod (I refer to this in chapter 11), but it does not countenance slapping, punching, kicking, throwing, or shoving our children. Such actions can only result in possible physical injury to our children and their loss of respect for us.

Most of us seem to forget that we can also injure our children by psychological abuse. Name-calling ("You dummy, you idiot, you clumsy fool"), an angry tone of voice, facial expressions, and a general attitude of displeasure with the child's presence ("You're always in my way!"), will drive our children from us. If we treated some close friends or neighbors the way we sometimes treat our children, we would be very lonely people.

3. *Fathers provoke their children by being absent.* I am convinced that an absentee father is one of the leading causes of anger in young men and women. When I speak of an absentee father, I mean not only the divorced father or the workaholic who is rarely home to see his wife or children. I am also referring to the father who, even when he is home, is so aloof or so absorbed in his own interests that he virtually ignores his family.

When a father is too busy watching the TV or reading the newspaper to answer his child's question, he is an absentee father. When a father fails to involve his children whenever possible in the necessary, daily activities around the home (e.g., a trip to the hardware store, weeding in the garden, cleaning out the garage), he is acting like an absentee father. I will never forget the times my father allowed me to go to work with him at his drugstore, or the hockey games we attended together, or the time we painted our large, gray, front veranda together. These kinds of activities with Dad spoke even louder than the words, "I love you." They said, "I love you enough to have you with me whenever possible."

David's neglect of Absalom (2 Sam. 14:28-29) led to some of the most painful experiences in the king's life. Eli's neglect of his sons resulted in their moral degeneration (1 Sam. 2:22). Fathers who fail to take the time to be with their children on a regular basis—to teach them, discipline them, play with them, and just to be their friend—run the risk of provoking their children to anger and driving them away from the faith.

In more and more homes children are being denied a father's love and guidance because of divorce. Ron Hutchcraft writes:

> The single parent is a new and growing challenge for the church. Twelve million children under the age of eighteen now live with a divorced parent. And that number is growing by one million each year.[2]

When the above quotation was written (1984), 90 percent of the single-parent families in the United States were headed by single mothers rather than single fathers.[3] Whether children are without a mother or a father, the very fact that they are being raised in a single-parent family increases the possibility of their developing an angry spirit. If they have been dragged through the painful experience of observing their parents separate and divorce or if they have been denied the love of one parent through death, they are forced to deal with situations that complicate their emotional stability and growth. Unless these children are constantly reassured of their remaining parent's love and given the support of their extended natural family and/or church family, they will, in all likelihood, have to deal with feelings of resentment, betrayal, and accompanying anger.

4. *We provoke our children with a tension-filled marriage.* Merton Strommen, in his book, *Five Cries of Youth*, writes:

> The most poignant cry is the sob of despair or shriek of sheer frustration among youth living in an atmosphere of parental hatred and distrust. Often it ends in running away from home, delinquent behavior, suicide, or other self-destructive behavior.[4]

Strommen is not exaggerating. Children want and need the security of a warm, loving, stable atmosphere. In my own conversations with young people I often ask the question, "What is the thing that upsets you the most in your home?" Invariably the answer is the same: "My parents arguing with each other." Young people idealize a family that is happy and unified. When the mother and father do not display these qualities, the children quickly lose hope. Ultimately, this frustration and hopelessness over family tensions can drive young people to seek some way of escape—be it drugs, an early marriage, running away, or suicide.

5. *We provoke our children with unclear and inconsistent parental expectations.* Children need to know what is expected of them and what will happen when they fail to meet those expectations. When the rules differ from one day to the next, when the form of punishment changes depending on the mood of the parents, when one child is favored over another, or when there is one set of standards for the parents and another set for the children, these in-

consistencies will cause our children to become angry. Adults don't like to be unsure about how to act or what will happen if they foul up. But for children to have to live every day of their entire childhood in that kind of uncertainty is cruel and unusual punishment to be sure.

In addition to these five probable causes, numerous other factors can provoke an angry spirit in our children: being too permissive with them, demanding more of them than they can give, etc. But the five actions listed above are the most likely to cause our children to become exasperated to the point of losing heart. As I have mentioned before, our children can be very forgiving and understanding. If we are provoking our children by one or more of these actions, we must seek our children's forgiveness, and we must change our ways. To continue in any of these patterns, knowing what they will do to our children, is sin on our part (James 4:17).

BRING THEM UP IN THE LORD

In the Ephesians 6:4 text, Paul not only gives the negative prohibition, but he also gives a positive directive. In true Pauline fashion (see Eph. 4:22-24) he tells fathers what to put off, and then he tells them what to put on. He says, "But bring them up in the discipline and instruction of the Lord."

The words *bring up* mean literally, "to feed" or "to nourish." Because the apostle contrasts these words with the words *provoke to anger*, he no doubt wants to stress the idea of tenderness and affection. The commentator William Hendriksen captures the idea best when he translates *bring up* as "rear them tenderly." Long before the insights of modern psychology, the Holy Spirit was instructing parents to treat their children as fragile, impressionable, sensitive creatures in need of tender, loving care. This kind of treatment, however, does not allow children to do as they please; it consists of "the discipline and instruction of the Lord."

The first word *discipline* (paideia) refers to training by the enforcement of rules and regulations. This enforcement may consist of rewards and, when necessary, punishments. It is the kind of training or discipline described by the author of Hebrews as seeming for the moment, not joyful, but sorrowful (Heb. 12:11). Not until children begin to enjoy the "peaceful fruit of righteousness" through an intelligent experience of the benefits of the Christian faith do they really appreciate the value and necessity of such training.

While the word *discipline* focuses more on what parents *do* to their children, the second word, *instruction* (nouthesia), focuses on what parents *say* to their children. The word means to train by verbal instruction for the purpose of bringing the child's behavior into line with God's revealed Word.[5] Most often it is translated as "admonishment" or, in the verbal form, "to admonish" (Col. 1:28; 3:16; Rom. 15:14).

This admonishment can involve words of encouragement or words of rebuke, blame, and correction. In 1 Samuel 3:13 the Lord told young Samuel that Eli's house would be judged forever "because his sons brought a curse on themselves and he did not rebuke them." The word for *rebuke* is *enouthetei* in the Septuagint—the common New Testament word for "admonish." The implication is that if Eli had been faithful to admonish and rebuke his sons concerning their behavior, they would not have grown up as profligates and rebels. Eli could very well have instructed his sons in the content of the revealed faith. His failure to rebuke and correct them is what the Lord singled out as the cause of His displeasure with the priest.

We must never think that simply communicating the facts of the Christian faith will be sufficient. In Colossians 1:28 Paul says, "And we proclaim Him, admonishing (noutheteo) every man and teaching (didasko) every man with all wisdom, that we may present every man complete in Christ." The task of bringing our children to the fullness of life in Christ definitely includes instruction in the details of the Christian faith. The word *teaching* (didasko) suggests the communication of information for the purpose of learning and remembering facts. This we do both formally and informally with our children. (I mentioned this in chapter 3, "Inculcate and Inoculate.") Paul's use of the word *admonish* (noutheteo), however, goes beyond the mere presentation of factual data. He implies that because the data already given is being misunderstood, misapplied, or ignored, there is a need for verbal correction. This is what Eli apparently failed to do with his sons. Unfortunately, it is also what many Christian fathers are failing to do today. And the consequences of their actions today do not differ from the consequences of the same actions in Eli's day.

Recently, I heard of a middle-aged man who had grown up in a preacher's home but rejected the faith which he had been taught from infancy. His father was a traveling evangelist who was rarely home to deal with his children. When he was home, he failed to discipline them according to the principles of Scripture. (I cover this in more detail in chapter 11, "Be Fair But Be Firm.") Today, the evangelist's son is on his third marriage, an alcoholic, and bitter toward the Christian faith.

The most significant part of the Apostle Paul's directive in Ephesians 6:4 is what he says at the end of the verse. He says we are to "bring them up in the discipline and instruction *of the Lord*"(emphasis added). This is what makes our child rearing distinctively Christian—it is "of the Lord." And this is what gives us hope that our training will lead our children to place their trust in Jesus Christ. In other words, it is not only training that is Christian (Christ-centered) as opposed to secular, but it is also training that involves the Lord's very presence and blessing. John Stott sums it up best when he says:

> Behind the parents who teach and discipline their children there stands the Lord Himself. It is He who

is the chief teacher and administrator of discipline. Certainly the overriding concern of Christian parents is not just that their children will submit to their authority, but that through this they will come to know and obey the Lord.[6]

To know that the Lord Himself stands behind us as we attempt to lead our children to Him ought to be a source of great comfort and encouragement. We are not bringing them up in the discipline and instruction of "ourselves" but "of the Lord." We may be very much involved in the process of leading our children to a personal knowledge of God, but it is the Lord alone who is directing that process. Therefore, let us always labor to follow His directives on parenting even if they seem to conflict with those that are commonly accepted by the world. If we train our children according to the Spirit of wisdom from above, not according to the wisdom of this world, we will succeed, hopefully, in leading them to an enduring faith in Jesus Christ.

For Review, Discussion, and Action:

1. Suggest at least two reasons why the Apostle Paul singles out the fathers in Ephesians 6:4 and Colossians 3:21.

2. How does it make you feel as a father (or as a mother) to know that fathers in particular are the object of this command?

3. Describe two different ways your children can express their anger. Do you detect either of these expressions of anger in your children already? If so, what are you going to do?

4. What are the five paternal (or parental) actions most likely to provoke anger in your children? For each of the five causes, rate yourself as to your present record of be-

havior. Would you score a *1* (never guilty), a *5* (occasionally guilty) or a *10* (frequently guilty)? Obviously, the higher the score the more serious the problem. When you have rated yourself, rate your spouse also. Then compare notes with each other.

5. Discuss the differences between the words *discipline* (paideia) and *instruction* (nouthesia) as used by Paul in Ephesians 6:4. List several ways you are presently engaging in both kinds of training with your children.

6. Illustrate how you have attempted (or will attempt) to teach and discipline your children so that your actions are "of the Lord" (Eph. 6:4).

For Further Study:

Adams, Jay E. *Competent to Counsel.* Phillipsburg: Presbyterian and Reformed Publishing Co., 1970. In this, his first of many books on biblical counseling, Dr. Adams sets forth the basic theory and technique of nouthetic counseling. His book contains one of the most consistent, biblically based approaches to problem solving on the market today.

Barnes, Robert G. *Single Parenting: A Wilderness Journey.* Wheaton: Tyndale House Publishers, Inc., 1984. This is one of many recent books on a Christian approach to single-parenting. The final chapter of the book, "The Unresponsive Child," is of special help for a single parent dealing with an angry child.

Hansel, Tim. *What Kids Need Most in a Dad.* Old Tappan: Fleming H. Revell Company, 1984. Tim Hansel has written a book to stimulate fathers to think through some of the myths about fatherhood and then take the time to plan how they can better fulfill the role of father.

Kesler, Jay, ed. *Parents and Teenagers*. Wheaton: Victor Books, 1984. This is a massive compendium of easy-to-read, topically arranged articles written by fifty of the nation's most respected Christian leaders on how to raise teenagers from a Christian perspective. I highly recommend this book for parents of adolescents or pre-adolescents.

MacArthur, John, Jr. *The Family*. Chicago: Moody Press, 1982. MacArthur has written a practical exposition of Ephesians 5:18–6:4 with an additional chapter on the divorce/remarriage question. He focuses on the Ephesians 6:4 passage in chapter 7.

Mack, Wayne. *How to Develop Unity in the Marriage Relationship*. Phillipsburg: Presbyterian and Reformed Publishing Co., 1977. This manual contains a wealth of biblical and practical material to help couples maintain unity in their marriages. On pages 115–128 the author gives us one of the most thorough explanations and practical applications of Ephesians 6:4 available.

Strommen, Merton P. *Five Cries of Youth*. San Francisco: Harper & Row, Publishers, 1974. Based on some of the most extensive research ever done on American church youth, this book covers what Strommen has concluded are the five most serious needs (cries) of teens. In chapter 3 he focuses on the cry of youth concerning family disunity. This is one book every parent and youth leader should read.

CHAPTER ELEVEN

BE FAIR BUT BE FIRM

Faith-formation Principle: To help our children come to an enduring faith in Christ, we must exercise the kind of discipline that is controlled by our unconditional love for them and reflects our sensitivity to their unique needs and personalities. Our discipline must also be firm enough to effect the desired change of behavior in our children and maintain our God-given, parental authority in the home.

Biblical Texts: Proverbs 22:15; 23:13-14

For seventeen years I pastored the Maple Glen Bible Fellowship Church, which is located in a fast-growing, middle-class, high-tech, suburban area ten miles north of Philadelphia. During my years at Maple Glen, I noticed that the number one concern of Christian parents remained basically the same: How should we best discipline our children?

Over the years numerous books have been written on the subject of disciplining children. Many authors claim to be treating the issue from a biblical perspective but, unfortunately, not all of them agree on the subject. This has only confused and frustrated parents who honestly desire to please God in the way they raise their children.

I do not propose to have the final answer on the subject of discipline. My wife and I have made our share of mistakes along the way (and still do), but God has graciously enabled us to persevere in the pattern or style of parenting which we believe is most in line with biblical principles. We are happy and grateful for the positive results of our efforts as evidenced in the lives of our three children to date. In particular, we are thankful for the clear indications of God's saving grace in each of their lives.

The subject of disciplining children can be approached from several different perspectives. We can discuss preventative discipline, which would include teaching our children self-discipline and responsibility. Or we can focus on discipline in terms of correcting or punishing the child's behavior. Our main emphasis in this chapter will be on corrective discipline as it relates to the final goal of leading our children to faith in Christ.

In the Youth Congress '85 Survey, I asked teenagers several questions about how they had been disciplined. Although the statistics failed to show any clear-cut patterns, I was able to make several broad generalizations:

(1) The form of discipline does have a measurable effect on the attitude of young people toward the Christian faith.

(2) Spanking and sending children to their rooms seem to have a more positive influence on their acceptance of the faith than do other forms of discipline (i.e., denying privileges, yelling, or nagging).

(3) Parents who take time to explain the reasons for the discipline will find their children more open to the Christian faith than those who do not explain the reason for their disciplinary action.

(4) Parents who are willing to ask forgiveness of their children when they have disciplined them unfairly or without self-control will have more success keeping their children in the faith than those parents who never seek forgiveness.

IDENTIFY YOUR STYLE OF PARENTING

The Scriptures clearly teach that God has given parents authority over their children (Ex. 20:12; Eph. 6:1). The way in which we exercise that authority, however, determines to a great extent the particular style of parenting we adopt as our own. I am convinced that of the three most basic approaches to parenting only one of them allows us to discipline our children with the assurance that God will honor our efforts to lead our children into an enduring faith in Christ.

Before we look at what I believe to be the most effective style of parenting, let us examine the other popular approaches.

Dictatorial parenting. The dictatorial or authoritarian method of parenting assumes that the parents' authority can be wielded like an iron sword. Unfortunately, this is a very popular method among professing Christian parents. Fritz Ridenour states that almost 30 percent of the teenagers he interviewed described their parents in authoritarian terms.[1]

Dictatorial or authoritarian parents tend to be quick to bark orders and to use the rod as their primary means of discipline. They rarely allow their children to explain their actions; indeed, they tend to believe that children should be seen and not heard. They think their own opinion is always correct, and they view their children's attempts to explain their own behavior as back talk and further defiance of their authority. Not always, but usually, dictatorial parents give little physical affection or positive encouragement to their children.

Typical expressions from the dictatorial parent are: "As long as you are living in this house, you will...."; "Don't you ever interrupt me when I'm talking to you...."; "You do what I say when I tell you to. Do you understand?"

Permissive parenting. Permissive parents are on the other end of the pendulum from the authoritarian ones. They easily concede to the whims and fancies, whimpers and whines of their children. They are long on loving their children (they think) and short on discipline. They tend only to *request* their children to do things, and when the children refuse to comply, they sigh and act like they have a terrible lot to bear in life. Generally, the permissive style of parenting leads to a very chaotic household where the children run the entire show. Typical expressions from such parents include: "Now you know you shouldn't act that way. Won't you stop . . . please?"; "OK, do what you want."

Authoritative parenting. The authoritative style of parenting is the one that, I believe, most clearly reflects the biblical directives for the discipline of children. It avoids the extremes of the other two styles. Unlike the dictatorial method, the authoritative method of parenting recognizes the individuality and rights of the child without at the same time abdicating the authoritative role of the parent, as is the case with the permissive approach.

The authoritative parent is one who is clearly in control of his children but also one who is willing to listen to their questions, suggestions, and pleas before taking disciplinary action. He is fair and reasonable, yet firm and consistent. In essence, it is the authoritative style of parenting that we have been describing in the previous ten chapters.[2]

Parents who seek to pattern their child discipline practices after the authoritative model will generally avoid the problems caused by the other two styles of parenting. For example, children reared by dictatorial parents will often rebel and leave home as soon as they can. Some will adopt the same tough, military approach to raising children that their parents followed, or they will go to the opposite extreme and become permissive parents. Children raised by permissive parents run the risk of becoming spoiled brats who always want and expect their own way.

Ridenour points out that children of both dictatorial and permissive parents usually have trouble in the real world, especially handling differences of opinion. They have never been taught by their parents how to handle dissent. Dictatorial parents don't allow their children to express their own opinions; permissive parents never disagree with their children. In either case, the children are denied the opportunity to learn how to deal with opposing viewpoints by being good listeners and speaking the truth in love. In the authoritative approach, however, children are encouraged to state their case, as well as to listen to and accept the parents' final judgment. As the title of this chapter states, the authoritative style is fair but firm.

Those of us seeking to follow the authoritative approach must admit that we are not always true to our convictions. Most of us have found ourselves being dictatorial on some occasions and permissive on others. Perhaps out of the kindness of our hearts (or laziness of our bodies) we allow our child to get away with something we generally would not ignore. At that point we are being permissive in our approach. But then, when the child continues to take advantage of our oversight, we explode and come down hard with the hand of the dictator. And, of course, if we are constantly given to this seesaw approach to parenting, we will do more damage than if we were consistently following only one of the extreme positions.

But why is the authoritative style of parenting the one that God seems to bless the most as a means of leading our children to trust in Him? I believe there are two specific reasons.

1. *The authoritative style of parenting most clearly reflects the way God deals with us when we are in need of chastening.* He is neither authoritarian nor permissive in His care over us. He is fair and firm. His discipline is always motivated by love for us (Heb. 12:6), intended for our own good (Heb. 12:10), and aimed at producing in us His holiness and the peaceful fruit of righteousness (Heb. 12:10-11). Only the authoritative style of parenting can truly reflect this kind of loving motivation and then, hopefully, produce holiness and righteousness in our children.

2. *The authoritative style of parenting most accurately discharges the authority that God gives to parents as His representatives.* The other two approaches abuse that power. We must remember that our parental authority is not an absolute authority. It is derived from God and delegated by Him. In reality, we are His representatives, called to be stewards over these gifts that He has entrusted to us (Ps. 127). Someday we shall give an account of how faithfully we have exercised that authority for our children's spiritual benefit (Matt. 18:5-6).

Only in the authoritative approach is God's authority over the child properly exercised through the parents. The dictatorial pattern abuses the authority structure because, in essence, parents assume the role of God. They may think they are acting as people under authority, but their failure to chasten in love violates God's own pattern of discipline. Permissive parents, on the other hand, abuse their parental authority by allowing the child to assume the role of God. In both of these extreme positions God is relegated to second-in-command. The following diagram clearly illustrates the situation.

Dictatorial	*Permissive*	*Authoritative*
Parent	Child	God
God	God	Parent
Child	Parent	Child

Our children should be taught that our authority is real authority because it is derived from God. When they disobey us, they are disobeying the clear command of God. As Paul puts it in Ephesians 6:1, "Children, obey your parents in the Lord, for this is right." It is right because it is God's established pattern of exercising His authority over children.

KNOW WHEN TO USE THE ROD

It is important that parents view the disciplining of their children as the exercise of divinely given authority, for which they will some day give an account. Furthermore, parents must be convinced in their own minds that the proper exercise of discipline is one of the primary means God uses to bring children to Himself.

In Proverbs 22:15 we are told: "Foolishness is bound up in the heart of a child; the rod of discipline will remove it far from him." The word *foolishness* is not simply a reference to a child's immature or silly behavior. The Hebrew word is used nineteen times in Proverbs and in each case portrays a morally insolent and stubborn person. He refuses good counsel (Prov. 1:7; 10:8; 12:15; 15:5) and is quick to quarrel (12:16; 20:3). Worst of all, he mocks at sin (14:9). It is this kind of foolishness that resides by nature in the hearts of our children. If it is not driven out by the rod of discipline, their souls will end up in hell. This is the clear teaching of our second text, Proverbs 23:13-14:

> Do not hold back discipline from the child, although you beat him with the rod, he will not die. You shall beat him with the rod, and deliver his soul from Sheol.

Much has been written for and against the use of the rod. Some writers suggest that the shepherd's rod was used primarily to guide the sheep, not to hit them. Accordingly, respected authors like Dr. Ross Campbell argue that corporal punishment should be used as a last resort.[3] Others say that using the rod at the first indication of disobedience will more quickly remove the "foolishness" of the child and be far less stressful on both child and parent. Dr. Paul Meier writes:

> The Bible clearly calls for reproof and spanking as ideal punishments for young children, and as a

psychiatrist I agree wholeheartedly, even though some psychiatrists would disagree. Spanking is quick, and then it's over. It's not long and drawn out. It's applying the "board of education to the seat of knowledge!" It occurs immediately after the offense, so the young child knows what he is getting punished for.[4]

I agree with Dr. Meier. One cannot read the Word of God, especially the Book of Proverbs, and not notice the primacy of spanking as a God-ordained means of correction. Even though the rod was used to guide the sheep, I cannot escape the overwhelming evidence that in the Scriptures it is also a symbol of punishment and divine wrath (Ps. 2:9; Isa. 10:5, Rev. 12:5).

Granted, as Dr. Campbell argues so convincingly in his book, *How to Really Love Your Child*, parents must be "constantly reexamining their own expectations of their child, making sure that their expectations are reasonable, considerate, and are in accordance with their child's age, level of development, and ability to respond."[5] I also agree with Dr. Campbell's emphasis on keeping our children's emotional tanks full by giving them unconditional love, proper eye contact, physical contact, focused attention, and careful verbal instruction. The problem comes when a child openly resists and challenges the parents' (and God's) authority. Campbell says spanking should be the last form of punishment used; the Word of God seems to say it should be the primary one.

With the increase of child abuse in this country, it is not hard to understand why some committed Christian leaders are reluctant to promote spanking as a form of child discipline. But, as horrible and as unacceptable as the physical abuse of children may be, we cannot ignore what God has said regarding the value of the rod. He has clearly promised us that it is one of the means that will rescue our children from eternal disaster. In Proverbs 19:18 Solomon writes, "Discipline your son while there is hope, and do not desire his death." Although Solomon in this verse makes no specific reference to the use of the rod in discipline, it is logical to assume, in light of all the other references to the rod in Proverbs, that its proper use is implied in this verse also. Under the Old Testament economy, a child who grew up to be a disobedient and rebellious son was to be taken out and stoned to death by the elders of the town (Deut. 21:18-21). Solomon seems to be saying, "If you parents do not begin early to discipline your child [with the rod], you will be a willing party to his death. If you *really* love him, you will discipline him diligently" (Prov. 3:12; 13:24).

FOLLOW GOD'S PATTERN OF DISCIPLINE

In the suggested reading list at the end of the chapter, I recommend several excellent books on the subject of child discipline. I encourage you to consult one or more of these for detailed help in carrying out the discipline of children at each age-level. For our present study we will look only at those principles that refer to how the authoritative parent can provide a *strong foundation* for fair but firm discipline.

These principles are patterned after the way God deals with us as His children. He does not discipline us in a vacuum but rather holds us responsible for what He has already revealed as His authoritative will. If we desire to follow His disciplinary model, we must seek to incorporate the following four principles into our authoritative dealings with our children.

1. *We must clearly communicate what we expect of our children.* The Lord informs us of the specific boundaries for our behavior in His Word. The Bible as a whole has been given to us for the purpose of teaching us how to live lives that are pleasing to God (2 Tim. 3:16-17). In particular, He has set forth specific commands and principles that clearly define the moral boundaries within which we may freely live. For instance, in Ephesians 5:3-4 He does not

simply say, "Don't be immoral," He spells out what He views as immorality. We are not left to drift along in ignorance as to what He expects of us.

In a similar fashion, we must communicate to our children what we expect of them in regard to their behavior. This means we must instruct them in the teachings of Scripture and also inform them of the rules of the household. And these rules must be clearly spelled out for children of all ages. If you tell your five-year-old child to clean out the flower garden, you will probably find all your tulips and other perennials lying in a pile of rubble along with the weeds. If you give your nine-year-old lunch money and simply tell him to buy a nourishing meal, he will likely interpret that as freedom to buy candy, potato chips, and soda. If you inform your fifteen-year-old that she must be in at a decent hour, she may come home at one in the morning. To be fair and firm with your children you must be clear as to what you expect of them.

2. *We must make as few boundaries as possible.* At times God's Word may appear to be one endless list of rules and regulations; however, Jesus Himself declared that the whole law was summed up in one word—LOVE—love for God and love for neighbor (Matt. 22:37-40). Even if we include the Ten Commandments and all the other directives of Jesus and the apostles, the specific commands of Scripture, when viewed from the perspective or motive of love, leave Christians plenty of room to freely exercise their own will in making moral decisions. We are not treated as moral robots.

We must follow God's example and set as few boundaries as possible in regard to what we expect of our children as they are growing up in the home. We will teach them to obey the commands of Scripture. In addition to that, we should decide what we expect of our children at any given stage of their development and then establish the boundaries within which they can freely function and beyond which they can expect to be punished.

Often we discipline our children on impulse rather than in accordance with a carefully thought-out plan. This can only lead us to be inconsistent and unfair and cause our children to become confused and bitter. It is impossible to enforce boundaries if we do not establish them beforehand. And the fewer boundaries we have, the less chances there are of infractions. Furthermore, the fewer number of rules we create for our children, the more opportunities we give them to learn how to think and make moral decisions on their own.

Obviously, when our children are young, we must have more rules and tighter regulations. With our toddlers, for instance, we will often find ourselves issuing the decree of Colossians 2:21: "Do not handle, do not taste, do not touch!" Because young children do not have the ability to discern between what is harmful and what is safe, we must make many decisions for them, whether they like it or not.

As our children grow older, however, they must learn how to assume responsibility for their own actions. This will mean fewer rules and increased freedoms. For example, some parents complain that they must always remind their teenagers to keep their bedrooms clean. Perhaps the nagging could be avoided if these parents simply established three broad boundaries: "You will make your bed each day; you will keep your clothes picked up and stored in their proper places; your allowance will depend on how faithfully you stay within those boundaries." Similarly, when parents give their child an allowance, they should not dictate how the child is to spend each penny. Rather, the guiding boundaries might be that a portion of it should be given to the Lord, a portion saved, and a portion spent as the child desires.

The parent must always have the final say, but as our children grow older, we must give them an increasing say in the nature of the boundaries themselves. When their opinions are taken seriously, we will undoubtedly discover that they are more willing to work within the established boundaries than if they had no input at all.

Excessive rules and regulations in the home will cause unnecessary tension, fear, and resentment in the hearts of our children, but they may also create in our children, ultimately, a distaste for the Word of God.

3. *We must give reasons for our boundaries.* If anyone has a right to say, "Do it because I say so!" it is the God of the universe. And yet, the Lord constantly condescends to us and explains *why* He desires us to act a certain way. He did it with His people, Israel (Deut. 23:14), and He does it with us as well (Rom. 13:1-2).

There is a sense in which our children should obey us simply because we say so. They should learn to honor our word because they respect us as their parents; however, we must remember that we are not just after obedience—the dictatorial parent can obtain that. What we desire is an obedience that grows out of a respect and love for us and that will ultimately be transferred to God. As we have discussed in previous chapters, our ultimate goal is to help our children come under the authority of Christ. To that end we must give them reasons for the way we expect them to act. Sooner or later they are going to want to know why they should trust in Christ and why they should obey Him. If they grow up thinking, "Mom and Dad don't have any good reasons for me to obey them," they will probably conclude: "I guess God doesn't have any good reasons for me to obey Him either."

I will never forget the first time I heard a sermon on the omnipresence of God. As a small child, I did not understand all the big, theological terms the preacher used, but when he said God saw everything I did, heard everything I said, and knew my every thought, I realized in my childish way that someday I would answer to God for my disobedience. I could maybe fool Mom and Dad, but I could never fool the all-seeing God. In that moment, without any awareness of what was happening, I began to transfer my allegiance from my parents to Christ, and I began to come under the authority of His Word as well as theirs. Obedience to Him and to them began to make more sense to me.

4. *We must establish negative and positive consequences for our children's behavior.* Again, the divine pattern is clear; God spells out for us both the judgments and the blessings that are attached to His moral commands (Deut. 28:2, 15; Gal. 6:7-8; Eph. 5:5; James 1:12). If He does this for us, should we not also be quick to inform our children of what will happen if they obey or disobey our commands?

Most parents are more apt to try controlling the behavior of their children by threatening punishment rather than by promising rewards. But God uses both incentives, and so should we. There is nothing unbiblical or unspiritual about developing a merit system for behavior, including chores around the house.[6] Nor is it unwise to heap praise on our children for a job well done. Biblical discipline, if it is to reflect God's dealings with us, must include not only the threat of consequences for disobedience but also the promise of rewards and compliments for obedience.

I trust that it is clear from our study in this chapter that God's dealings with us, as His children, reveal a style of parenting most closely expressed by the authoritative model. Parents who follow either the dictatorial or permissive models will tend to abuse the authority God gives them. Only the authoritative style accurately discharges that authority. It alone provides a model of parenting that is both fair and firm.

For Review, Discussion, and Action:

1. With which of the three different styles of parenting do you identify? Was this a deliberate choice? Why?

2. What is the meaning of Proverbs 22:15: "Foolishness is bound up in the heart of a child"? Give examples of this foolishness as you have observed it in your own children.

3. Christians disagree about the using the rod to discipline children. Using the following verses as a basis for your argument, write a short paragraph describing your understanding of the biblical view of corporal punishment: 2 Sam. 7:14; Prov. 10:13, 13:24, 22:15, 23:13-14, 29:15; 1 Cor. 4:21.

4. What are four specific principles necessary to provide a strong foundation for fair but firm discipline of your children? How do God's dealings with His people provide the model for each of these four principles? Which of these principles are you presently putting into practice?

5. If you haven't already done so, write down the major rules in your home as they relate to your children. Explain the reasons for these rules to your children, making sure they understand the consequences for obedience and disobedience.

For Further Study:

Adams, Jay E. *Christian Living in the Home.* Grand Rapids: Baker Book House, 1972. In chapter 8, "Discipline with Dignity," Dr. Adams examines both the abuses and proper exercise of biblical discipline. He also provides a simple form which parents can use in order to lay out a code of conduct for their children.

Campbell, Ross. *How to Really Love Your Child.* Wheaton: Victor Books, 1977. Although I disagree with Campbell's negative attitude toward the use of the rod, I recommend this book for its clear emphasis on loving your child as part of the disciplinary process.

Christenson, Larry. *The Christian Family.* Minneapolis: Bethany House Publishers, 1970. This is one of the best general books on the family I have ever read. The author's treatment of child discipline (pp. 91-125) makes a compelling appeal for the use of the rod as the first resort, not the last.

Dobson, James. *Dare to Discipline*. Wheaton: Tyndale House Publishers, 1970. Dr. Dobson's popular book has done much to counteract the permissive approach to discipline that produced the generation of the sixties. His arguments are more pragmatically based (they work; therefore, they are right) than grounded in Scripture; however, his book is most helpful as a guide to teaching our children to respect authority.

Fennema, Jack. *Nurturing Children in the Lord*. Phillipsburg: Presbyterian and Reformed Publishing Co., 1978. This book is aimed primarily at helping teachers follow a biblical approach to discipline in the classroom, but its content is equally applicable for parents in the home.

Mack, Wayne. *How to Develop Deep Unity in the Marriage Relationship*. Phillipsburg: Presbyterian and Reformed Publishing Co., 1977. On pages 127-130 Dr. Mack gives a brief but helpful outline of the main principles of discipline.

Meier, Paul D. *Christian Child-Rearing and Personality Development*. Grand Rapids: Baker Book House, 1977. Basing most of what he says on psychological theory, Meier attempts to weave biblical principles into his philosophy of child rearing. Generally this is a very helpful overview of the psychological growth of children. Discipline is discussed in line with the various stages of growth.

Ray, Bruce A. *Withhold Not Correction*. Phillipsburg: Presbyterian and Reformed Publishing Co., 1978. This is one of the most thorough works available on discipline from a biblical perspective. Of special help is chapter 6, in which the author deals with love and the use of the rod.

Ridenour, Fritz. *What Teenagers Wish Their Parents Knew about Kids*. Waco: Word Books, 1982. In chapter 8 Ridenour focuses on the strengths and weaknesses of the three styles of parenting.

Stanley, Charles. *How to Keep Your Kids on Your Team*. Nashville: Oliver Nelson Publishers, 1986. In chapter 5 Dr. Stanley gives some excellent guidelines for establishing parameters of behavior in the home.

Strommen, Merton P. and Irene A. *Five Cries of Parents*. San Francisco: Harper & Row, Publishers, 1985. A companion book to *Five Cries of Youth*, this latest work focuses on how parents should prepare for and make the most of their children's adolescent years. On page 145 the authors discuss the authoritative style of parenting and its positive effect on our children's moral values and beliefs.

CHAPTER TWELVE

MODEL THE "LIGHT LOAD"

Faith-formation Principle: *To help our children come to an enduring faith in Christ we must introduce them to* **true** *Christianity by modeling a faith that offers an easy yoke and a light load.*

Biblical Text: Matthew 11:29-30
As I have stated in a previous chapter, I am convinced that many of our young people are being alienated from the Christian faith, not because they are opposed to the teachings of historic Christianity, but because they are turned off by the lives of the adults who profess to believe these teachings. The fact is, they have not really seen *true* Christianity in operation. What they have observed in much of the evangelical sector is a narrow, pharisaical, distorted expression of the faith. Consequently, by the time they enter their teen years they have begun to develop either an attitude of indifference or a spirit of resentment toward Christianity.

In Matthew 11:28-30 Jesus gives one of the most gracious invitations in all of Scripture. He invites sinners to find rest from their burdens by taking His yoke upon them, a yoke which He describes as easy and light. It is this yoke that we as Christian parents long to see our children adopt as their own, for it is a yoke of identification with Christ. It is a call to Christian discipleship, to membership in the school of Christ. As Jesus Himself said, "Take My yoke upon you, and *learn* from Me" (v. 29, emphasis added).

The most fascinating feature of this invitation, however, is the promise attached to it. Generally, we think of a yoke as a heavy, burdensome thing. It is something that slows us down and binds us to hard labor. But Jesus says His yoke is "easy" and His load is "light" (v. 30). He promises to give "rest" to those who are "weary and heavy-laden" if they take His yoke on them (v. 28).

We must not forget the context in which Jesus gave this invitation. The Pharisees, for many years, had been laying heavy burdens on the people. They taught people that the only way they could have relief from the weight of their sins was to keep the laws and traditions of their forefathers. But this works-related righteousness only heaped a greater burden on them (Matt. 23:4; Acts 15:10). So Jesus' message would indeed stand in stark contrast to that of the Pharisees.

It is my conviction that one of the more subtle, unspoken causes behind the alienation of our young people from the faith is the heavy, unpleasant burdens we have often placed on them by our pharisaical interpretation of the Scriptures and by our rigid, rule-controlled lifestyles. As we observed in chapter 4, we have often majored on our lists of do's and don'ts and ignored the need for a heart-religion. In a sense, we have been like the blind leaders of the blind. Our children have looked to us as the religious authorities in their lives, but we have failed them by stressing the externals, rather than communicating the spirit of the Law and the heart of true religion. As a result, many of them have been influenced by their peers and by the world in general to turn their backs on Christianity.

In particular, we have placed unnecessary burdens on

our young people by our failure to do at least three things.

(1) We have failed to model a sense of the joy involved in living the Christian life.

(2) We have failed to communicate by our example the spirit of compassion and service to the needy that is the heart of true Christianity.

(3) We have failed to maintain open minds that enable us to deal lovingly with our children's questions and honest doubts.

MODEL THE JOY OF LIFE IN CHRIST

In the preceding eleven chapters, we have discussed principles that affect the training of our children at every age and stage of their growth. Although the same can be said for the principle we will consider in this chapter, our focus of attention is especially on adolescents and teenagers.

Teenagers, in general, love to have fun. They enjoy being happy and carefree. In a recent nationwide study, 3,600 Canadian teenagers revealed that friendships (74 percent) and music (72 percent) were their two most popular sources of enjoyment.[1] Wise Christian parents and educators will learn from these statistics and establish appropriate priorities to minister to their own young people. We should be helping teenagers develop discernment in the kinds of friends they make and in the music they listen to. In our churches we should be more sensitive to these built-in needs of our teens. I am not advocating punk-rock hymn-sings or heavy-metal accompaniment, but I am suggesting a willingness, at least, to do some creative thinking as to how we can better minister to the needs of our teens in the total church program, including the worship services.

When Jesus says in our text, "My yoke is easy," He is saying that His yoke is something pleasant and delightful. It is not a dull, heavy burden to be borne but a relationship that sets men free to enjoy all of life as never before. I wonder, are our children getting the impression, as they grow up in our homes, that Christianity provides a pleasant way of life? Or are they being taught by the example of their parents that Christianity is a duty and that it is the material things of this world that really make us happy?

Are our children learning from our involvement in the activities at church and from our relationships with other believers that knowing and serving Christ is a source of great happiness and joy? Or are we teaching them that the Christian faith is to be identified with long, dull, sullen, somber worship services and with people who rarely smile or have a good laugh about anything?

Fortunately, our churches today do contain a lot of happy, joyful believers, and a good number of young people are finding true happiness in Jesus Christ. In fact, Merton Strommen discovered such a deep-felt expression of joy and happiness among the 7,000 churched young people he surveyed that he labeled it one of the five cries of youth. He writes:

> Joy pulsates this fifth cry. It may take the form of quiet exuberance over the simple pleasures of living. Or it may be a shout of celebration and hope that contrasts with the despair and cynicism so often heard from twentieth century man. It is the cry of youth whose joy is in a sense of identity and mission that centers in the person of Jesus Christ.[2]

True joy, of course, is something beyond being happy. It is a fruit of the Spirit that enables believers to be content even in times of sorrow and suffering. Jesus, for the *joy* set before Him endured *the cross* (Heb. 12:2, emphasis added). He was a man of sorrows and acquainted with grief (Isa. 53:3) but also a man who wanted His joy to be made full in us (John 15:11). Joy, then, is the attitude that enables us to be glad to be alive in good times and in bad. It rests, not on circumstances, but on our confidence in God's love for us in every circumstance (Rom. 8:28).

Even though Christian joy is not to be equated with happiness or having fun or a good laugh, it is most certainly not opposed to those things. Indeed, I am convinced that only Christians who have the joy of Jesus in their hearts can really know what it means to be happy. In other words, if ever a home should be full of laughter, it should be the home of a Christian family. If ever a gathering of people should sense the pure delight of being with friends, it should be saints assembled for worship or united together for ministry.

I plead with you parents to make your home a happy, fun-filled place. Show your children that loving and serving Jesus is not dull and burdensome but rather the most pleasant and delightful thing they could ever do. Learn to laugh a lot. Rejoice always. You will discover that your children enjoy being around you and that they enjoy bringing their friends home with them. Most of all, you will find that your children will be open to learning of the One who has made life so full of joy for Mom and Dad.

In the helpful book, *What They Did Right*, Elisabeth Elliot and thirty-eight other Christians explain how their parents' lives influenced them to become Christians. After describing her rather strict, religious upbringing, Elisabeth Elliot concludes her testimony with these words:

> If the picture seems, as it will to some, anything but ideal, and perhaps incredibly rigorous and austere, I know that any one of the six of us children would be glad to testify to the rollicking fun we have always had. We got together again, thirty of us, in 1972, and for a week most of us were laughing most of the time.[3]

MODEL A SPIRIT OF SERVICE TO OTHERS

One of the most often ignored characteristics of young people, especially those in the mid-to-late teens, is their concern over injustice in the world and an accompanying

desire to do something to correct it. In the sixties and early
seventies, for example, this inner struggle led to violent,
outward expression on our college campuses. It was right
in the middle of this period of turmoil that Merton
Strommen conducted his survey of 7,000 churched young
people. It should not surprise us that his research led him
to include the "Cry of Social Protest" as one of the five
cries of youth. Although young Americans in the sixties
were especially vocal about their frustrations with the war
in Vietnam and the social injustices in America, their outbursts of anger revealed a common element in all developing young people.

Strommen suggests that most young people are: (1) hu-
manitarian, (2) oriented to change, (3) socially involved,
(4) concerned over national issues, and (5) critical of the
institutional church, in which adults seem not to be caring.[4]
Strommen admits his studies show that, "many of the socially concerned are solid humanists who do not believe in
the Gospel," but he also adds, "An equal proportion of the
youth . . . reflect a knowledge of the Christian faith and a
love for their church."[5] Today, also, the present generation
of church youth are expressing a similar social concern.
The next time you observe a Pro-Life march take note how
many participants are teens and college students. Consider
also the number of young people who are going on short-
term missions projects in poverty-stricken urban and rural
areas.

Not all young people, of course, demonstrate this concern for the welfare of others. In fact, the generation of the
late seventies and eighties seems to be more concerned
about providing for its own needs. The hippies have given
way to the yuppies. And yet the spirit of idealism does
remain in the hearts of some of our young people. As
Christian parents and church leaders, we must be on the
lookout for its every appearance. We must not try to
smother it or discourage it, but rather we must guide it into
the right channels of service. If we don't, the world will.

Our children especially need to see in us a reflection of the servant spirit of Christ Himself. The call to take up the yoke of Jesus is a call to join the Master in service to others. Jesus told His disciples, "The Son of Man did not come to be served, but to serve, and to give His life a ransom for many" (Mark 10:45). He expects His disciples to show the same kind of compassion and mercy that He did while He was here on earth. In fact, Jesus teaches us that it is the disciple who is willing to give of himself to others, in acts of love and kindness, who engages in "pure and undefiled religion" (James 1:27). In Christ's eyes, the willing servant is the greatest in the kingdom of heaven (Luke 22:25-27). By his deeds of mercy he is actually showing kindness to Christ Himself (Matt. 25:31-46).

It is, therefore, incumbent on Christian parents and church leaders to help young men and women direct their energies into worthy deeds of compassion. We must begin by listening to their complaints and even helping them express their concerns. They need our sympathetic ears, not our condemning tongue. We must also be modeling the servant spirit for them by our own involvement in ministries of mercy. When our children see us defending the rights of the downtrodden, taking in the homeless, and clothing the poor, they will see true faith at work (James 2:14-17). They will say to themselves, "If this is true Christianity, I'm for it." But if we who have been the objects of God's mercy and grace ignore the injustices in society and turn our backs on the needs of the hurting people of this world, then we should not be surprised when our children become disillusioned with us and with the Christian faith.

BE WILLING TO DEAL WITH DOUBTS

One of the common complaints of young people raised in Christian homes is that their parents tend to have closed minds. These parents, most of whom follow a dictatorial style of parenting, just refuse to discuss certain topics with their children. They tend to hold to rigid, clear-cut views and are not open to being challenged by anyone, especially their children. However, all parents are susceptible to the charge of being closed-minded if they try to avoid the hard questions.

It is important for us to realize that Jesus never turned away a serious inquirer (John 3:4; Luke 18:18). Nor should we. The Apostle Peter tells us we are to be ready to make a defense to everyone who asks us to give an account for the hope that is in us (1 Peter 3:15). Surely, the "everyone" includes our children. Be it the inevitable "Who made God?" type of questions from our five-year-old or the "What's wrong with premarital sex?" type of questions from our fifteen-year-old, we must be ready and willing to give an answer.

One of the greatest fears of Christian parents is that their children will begin to doubt the tenets of the faith. And, ironically, some of those who fear the most are the very parents who refuse to talk to their children about their doubts. These parents seem to believe that their children are guilty of sin if they question any part of the Christian faith.

But parents must understand that one of the primary ways children learn is by asking questions. What parents of a four-year-old have not had times when they thought the only word the child knew was *why*? The fact is, our teens are still asking *why*. When their inquiries focus on moral values or on issues of religious faith, we should not go into a state of shock or become paranoid with fear, thinking our children are about to reject Christianity. Their questions are most likely the result of honest and healthy reflection on facts that, until the present, they had always accepted as true simply because Mom and Dad told them they were true. If our children are ever going to internalize these facts, they must understand and believe them because of personal conviction, not just because of parental persuasion.

In recent years, developmental psychologist James

Fowler has made significant contributions in the area of faith development. Although I cannot accept his definition of faith—he views true faith as a natural development in all men—I believe Fowler's insights into the characteristics of faith at each of the various stages of development are most helpful.[6] Regarding the Individuative-Reflective stage, which begins with young adults, he writes:

> It is in this transition that the late adolescent or adult must begin to take seriously the burden of responsibility for his or her own commitments, life-style, beliefs, and attitudes.[7]

Fowler is saying that it is *natural* for young people to begin to feel responsible for their own belief-system. When our teens begin to question the value or the necessity or even the moral correctness of things we have been teaching them all their lives, we should not immediately regard their actions as the beginnings of a rebellious spirit. Rather, we should view their actions as further proof of their transition into the next stage of faith development.

Strommen points out that in the New Testament the Greek word for *doubt* can be used in either a positive or a negative sense.[8] Negatively, the word suggests a rebellious attitude and/or lack of faith in God. This use of the word does not refer to questions of inquiry or a search for the truth but rather to expressions of unbelief, which flow not from an open-minded heart but from a double-minded or closed-minded one (James 1:6-8).

Positively, and most frequently, the word *doubt* is translated "to discern, to distinguish, to examine." The word conveys the idea of someone who is eager to be convinced of something for himself and is open to hearing all sides of the issue. I believe that often it is this kind of doubt that our teens are experiencing as they seek to develop a life-philosophy of their own. As Merton and Irene Strommen put it:

Doubt can become a plus in conversations about faith. An adolescent's doubts usually are rooted in a need for answers. Doubt can be a state of open-mindedness in which faith is asking the intellect for help.[9]

Let's face the facts, parents. Our teenagers are going to confront us with some hard questions. What a tragedy if, by our own closed-mindedness to their legitimate open-mindedness, we drive them away to the world for the answers that can be found only in the Gospel (2 Peter 1:3).

STEER AWAY FROM EXCESSSIVE RULES

One of young people's principle concerns is moral behavior. Society at large tells them there are no revealed moral absolutes. They all must decide for themselves the standards by which they are going to live. On the other hand, most children raised in the church are taught that God has clearly set forth certain standards of morality and that failure to abide by these rules or commandments will bring down His judgment. Some parents and churches go far beyond the biblical standards and add a list of their own rules and regulations which they impose on themselves and their children as if they also were given from above.

It ought not to shock us that young people who have been raised in this kind of rule-oriented atmosphere struggle when they are bombarded with the world's open-minded approach to morality. Unless they have some very good reasons for keeping the rules they have been taught at home, many of them will cave in under the pressure of the appeal of the world. In other words, if they have not been receiving spiritual inoculations as they have been growing up, and if their consciences have not been trained by biblical principles of wisdom, then it is highly probable that their natural, fleshly desires (and hormones) will concede to the "wisdom" of the world's standards.

The Pharisees were masters at placing heavy burdens on

the people by imposing on them myriads of rules. Often, young people raised in fundamentalist Christian homes complain of a similar burden. Many are forsaking the faith as a result.[10] Obviously, living by rule-keeping is not the pattern God promises to honor. That does not mean Christians ignore God's revealed moral laws; however, parents who really want to prepare their children to make wise decisions when they reach adolescence must begin to teach them the biblical principles of wisdom when they are young. Parents ought to emphasize a wisdom-oriented life rather than a rule-oriented life.

The Scriptures say a great deal about wisdom and its special value for youth. (See Proverbs 3:21-22.) In Proverbs 9:10 Solomon tells his son: "The fear of the Lord is the beginning of wisdom, and the knowledge of the Holy One is understanding." All Christian parents desire this for their children. We all long to see our sons and daughters come to a personal, saving knowledge of God through faith in His Son, Jesus Christ (John 17:3). We all look for evidence of a fear of God in their lives—not a fear that causes them to run from God, as Adam and Eve did, but a fear that leads them to love, obey, and serve Him.

To fear God means to live a pure and godly life (Ps. 19:9). Solomon says it is the beginning or, literally, the essence, the core of life. In other words, the education of our children is *Christian* education only as it is grounded in, and permeated by, the wisdom of God. This wisdom is found in God's Word, both written (1 Cor. 2:6-16) and incarnate (1 Cor. 1:30). It does not consist only of understanding certain facts, but also involves the application of those facts to the way we live. Biblical wisdom affects our moral behavior; it governs our entire lifestyle (Eph. 5:15-17). That is why we must make it the foundation of our children's training. When they are taught from the perspective of God's wisdom instead of the perspective of the world's wisdom, they will be able to make wise decisions as they weather the turbulent years of adolescence. They may still have many questions and maybe even some doubts, but they will not be weighed down with heavy burdens of a Christianity that is characterized by unnecessary externals.

The goal of our parenting is to fashion our children into Christian decision-makers. To do this we must seek to place the yoke of Christ on them. God alone can make them into true Christians, but we are responsible to keep them in that sphere of Gospel influence that will be most likely to woo their hearts and minds to Christ.

One of the primary reasons young people reject the faith is the pressure they experience from their peers and non-Christian friends. At times that pressure can be overpowering, especially for young people who have not yet experienced true freedom and joy in Christ by being placed under His yoke. We can help our children take the yoke of Christ on them so they can enjoy true freedom and wisdom in this life. What our young people are looking for as they reach adolescence is a religion that communicates a spirit of joy, an attitude of compassion and justice to the downtrodden, and a willingness to openly discuss the hard questions of life. The only way we can meet these needs in our teenagers is to teach them, from the very beginning, to view all of life according to the biblical principles of wisdom. When we faithfully help them to come to a fear of God and a knowledge of the Holy One, we are setting them on the path that will most likely lead them to an enduring faith in Christ.

For Review, Discussion, and Action:

1. Jesus says in Matthew 11:30 that His yoke is easy and His load is light. As your children observe you living the Christian life, what specific things could they see that demonstrate the truth of Christ's words? What could they see in your life that might lead them to think His yoke is burdensome?

2. What is the difference between being happy and being joyful?

3. Complete the following sentence: I express joy in Jesus by
   a. _____
   b. _____
   c. _____

4. List five things you can do or are already doing to show to your children that you are concerned about injustice, poverty, etc.

5. Why do you think so many parents are afraid to talk to their teens about moral issues and religious doubts?

6. Discuss with your children the subject of wisdom, using such verses as Proverbs 2:6-7; 3:13-14, 21-22; 14:16; 1 Corinthians 1:30; James 1:5-6. If they are old enough to understand, ask them if they currently view Christianity in terms of keeping rules or in terms of learning biblical principles for godly living.

For Further Study:

Adams, Jay E. *Back to the Blackboard*. Phillipsburg: Presbyterian and Reformed Publishing Co., 1982. In chapter 7 Dr. Adams discusses the issues of doubt and wisdom, among many others issues, as they relate to the final product of Christian education.

Bibby, Reginald W. and Posterski, Donald C. *The Emerging Generation*. Toronto: Irwin Publishing, 1985. This book is a well-written documentary on the state of Canada's teenagers. It touches on the need to give young people "room to emerge" (pp. 112–126) and deals with their sources of enjoyment (pp. 29–49).

Hearn, Virginia, ed. *What They Did Right*. Wheaton: Tyndale House Publishers, Inc., 1974. In this very readable book, thirty-nine believers give testimony as to how their parents influenced them to follow the Christian faith.

Stanley, Charles. *How to Keep Your Kids on Your Team*. Nashville: Oliver Nelson Publishers, 1986. Dr. Stanley gives some very helpful insights into how to teach the principle of wisdom to our children (chapter 10).

Strommen, Merton P. *Five Cries of Youth*. San Francisco: Harper & Row Publishers, 1974. The author deals with the importance of joy in the lives of young people (chapter 6), the importance of having compassion (chapter 4), and the importance of an open mind (chapter 5).

CHAPTER THIRTEEN

PRAY! PRAY! PRAY!

Faith-formation Principle: *To help our children come to an enduring faith in Christ, we must pray that God will help us diligently apply the twelve faith-formation principles so that our children will indeed come to a saving knowledge of Jesus Christ and serve Him as Lord of their lives all their days.*

Biblical Text: 1 Samuel 12:23
In chapter 3 we discussed the four most compelling reasons for faith rejection according to the Youth Congress '85 questionnaire. Each of these reasons in some way relates to the negative influence of the world's philosophy and lifestyle on the thinking and behavior of our children. The faith-formation principles we have considered in this book provide a biblical response to the world's influence. However, simply understanding the principles and agreeing that they are biblically based is not enough. We must actively apply these principles to the lives of our children. Indeed, there is a sense in which we must labor at the parenting task as if the salvation of our children rested on our faithfulness alone. At the same time we must depend totally on

the mercy of God to bless our efforts and save and keep our children in accordance with His own sovereign, gracious will.

From whatever perspective we choose to view the rearing of our children, either from God's sovereignty or from our own responsibility, one thing is certain—we must pray. We must pray that God will help us to be faithful in applying these important faith-formation principles, and we must pray that He will honor the promises of His Word and graciously save our children through these God-ordained means. Without prayer, we can only hope in the flesh. But if we learn to cry out to God for His wisdom and strength, we can go about our parenting duties with the confidence that our labors will not be in vain in the Lord.

God's people have always had to struggle against the evil influence of the world. As we discussed in chapter 4, Satan, as the god of this age, works through the lust of the flesh, the lust of the eyes, and the pride of life to draw God's people away from the path of obedience. He has always worked that way. In the days of Samuel, Israel cried out for a king. Even though, as a theocracy, they had the God of the universe as their monarch, they were not satisfied. They wanted to be "like all the nations" (1 Sam. 8:5-7). In other words, the pressures of the world's ways tempted them to reject God's way.

In 1 Samuel 12, aged Samuel rebukes the people for asking for a king, and God confirms the prophet's word with thunder and lightening. When the people cry out in fear and ask Samuel to pray that God will have mercy on them for their worldly desires, the prophet assures them that if they turn away from the futile things and follow the Lord with all their hearts, God will not abandon them. And then he adds:

> Moreover, as for me, far be it from me that I should sin against the Lord by ceasing to pray for you; but I will instruct you in the good and right way. Only

fear the Lord and serve Him in truth with all your
heart; for consider what great things He has done
for you (1 Sam. 12:23-24).

Samuel viewed his responsibility as twofold: (1) he had
to pray for the people, and (2) he had to teach them how to
live the good and right way. Teaching and praying. Praying
and teaching. Not either/or, but both/and. Indeed, he realized that these duties were so central to his role as the
prophet of Israel that to neglect either of them would be to
"sin against the Lord." Parents, do you feel that way about
your responsibility to your children? Do I? We should.

God has made us as parents to be prophets, kings, and
priests within our own families. As prophets we must instruct our children in the Word of God. As kings we must
exercise His rule over them. But as priests we must diligently pray for His saving grace to be imparted to them.
With Samuel, we must say to each of our children, "Far be
it from me that I should sin against the Lord by ceasing to
pray for you; but I will instruct you in the good and right
way."

Many times, as a small child, I would walk into my parents' room in the late evening to find them both kneeling
beside the bed praying. Almost every morning during my
teenage years I remember seeing my dad in the rocking
chair in the den, his big, tattered Bible in one hand and his
even bigger Matthew Henry Commentary in the other. Often his head was bowed in prayer. Once his cheeks were
wet with tears. I suspect that my older brother and I were
the objects of many of those parental prayers and tears. I
do know this, though: just the act of observing my parents'
faithfulness in prayer was a very powerful influence in my
life.

But how should we actually pray for our children? I
would like to suggest three characteristics of parental
prayers as illustrated by the example of parents in
Scripture.

PRAY REDEMPTIVELY

Parents should pray for their children redemptively. I do not mean by that expression that our prayers can merit the salvation of our children. What I do mean is that because God has placed the children of believers within the very special sphere of Gospel influence (1 Cor. 7:14) and has promised to include them in the blessings of the new covenant (Acts 2:39; Heb. 9:15), parents have every right to pray with confidence for the salvation of their children. We should pray for God to forgive them of their sins.

In Job 1:5 we read that whenever Job's children would feast together, their father would "send and consecrate them, rising up early in the morning and offering burnt offerings according to the number of them all; for Job said, 'Perhaps my sons have sinned and cursed God in their hearts.' Thus Job did continually." Job was concerned about the salvation and the spiritual needs of his children. In offering up sacrifices for their potential sins, he was acting redemptively in accordance with the revealed pattern of his day.

Today we do not have to slaughter sacrifices for the sins of our children; instead, we must offer up sacrifices of prayer on their behalf. We must ask God to forgive them for their sin and keep them from the destructive ravages of sin by covering them with the blood of Jesus Christ. Like Job, however, there may be certain occasions when we must be especially watchful in prayer for our sons and daughters. Andrew Murray writes:

> Every thoughtful parent knows there are times and places when the temptations of sin come more speedily and more easily surprise even the well-disposed child. Such are the times, both before and after a child goes into the company and the circumstances where he may be tempted, that a praying father and mother should do what Job did when he sent for his sons and sanctified them.[1]

Before my oldest daughter left for her first semester of living on a secular college campus, I consecrated her by praying with her and asking God to cover her with the protective power of the blood of Christ. Even though she has a close walk with the Lord and desires to share her love of Him with others on campus, I cannot ignore the fact that she is going into the front lines of Satan's territory. She needs the full panoply of spiritual armor that God has promised His own, especially the weapon of prayer (Eph. 6:18).

Although I believe God's dealings with His people in the new covenant are on an individual basis (I refer to this in chapter 2), I also share the conviction of many of my Presbyterian brothers that there is a sense in which the father is a steward of God's grace to his children. I do not feel free to baptize infants as a sign of their membership in the covenant because I am convinced that the spiritual nature of the new covenant presupposes faith prior to baptism; yet, I understand that the father's priestly role in the family does give him the right and the responsibility to plead his children's case before the throne of God. I believe I am responsible to pray for the sanctification of my children (and of my wife) on a regular basis. As the Scriptures say of Job, "Thus Job did continually." The fact is, all godly and loving parents (whatever their theological distinctives may be) will not have to be encouraged to pray for their children's spiritual needs. Their love for their offspring will compel them to pray redemptively—continually.

PRAY PERSEVERINGLY
There will be times for most of us Christian parents when we will wonder if our application of these faith-formation principles is having any positive impact on our children. And there will be times when we will question the efficacy of our prayers for our children. Their attitudes toward spiritual things and their behavior in general will leave us totally frustrated with being a parent, and we will wish we

could just escape for a while. Am I right? It is on occasions such as this that you must pray perseveringly for your children.

One day a Canaanite woman came to Jesus pleading with Him to heal her demon-possessed daughter (Matt. 15:21-28). Jesus' response to her was one of total silence. Matthew records: "He did not answer her a word" (v. 23). This only caused her to shout all the more so that the disciples finally came to Jesus and begged Him to get rid of the woman.

In the exchange of conversation that followed between Jesus and the woman, we see a beautiful illustration of persevering prayer. It is similar to the account of the importunate widow pleading her case before the unjust judge. Luke states that "He [Jesus] was telling them a parable to show that at all times they ought to pray and not lose heart" (Luke 18:1). Prayer is faith-oriented communing with the living Christ. The Canaanite woman brought her requests to Jesus in the flesh; we plead with Him through the Spirit. But in both cases there is communion with the living God. We ought to be no less persistent in seeking God's best for our children than this Canaanite woman was. She kept pleading her case for her daughter no matter what obstacle, argument, or seeming contempt she encountered. She met every negative response with more faith. I believe this woman knew deep down in her heart that Jesus would not deny her serious request for her daughter's deliverance. She had heard about His miraculous deeds. She saw compassion in His eyes. She would not be denied.

Have you ever felt that desperate about your children? I doubt any of us have ever had a demon-possessed child (despite what we might think of their behavior). But most of us have had, or will have, occasions to be greatly concerned about the spiritual status of our children. Even after they have professed faith in Christ, we will see habits or behavior patterns in their lives that will grieve our souls and cause us to wonder if they really know God. What should we do when that happens—just pray? No! Our prayers for them must be accompanied by a willingness to confront them concerning their spiritual inconsistencies.

In Galatians 6:1 we read that "if a man is caught in any trespass, you who are spiritual, restore such a one in a spirit of gentleness; each one looking to yourself, lest you too be tempted." If our children are the ones who appear to be caught in (trapped or overwhelmed by) a trespass (i.e., constant disobedience to parents), we must confront them about it. However, we must first remember our own weaknesses. The fact that we may be more "spiritual" does not mean we are invulnerable to falling into sin ourselves.

Some time ago two of my children got into a heated argument over some obtuse rule in the Monopoly game they were playing. Their "spiritual" father finally intervened by loudly rebuking their sinful behavior and impatiently quoting several pertinent Scripture verses. In other words, I totally blew it. I did not confront them in a "spirit of gentleness," nor did I "look to myself lest I too was tempted." The point of this little digression is simply this—when we see patterns of sinful behavior developing in our children, we must deal with them on two fronts: (1) we must pray perseveringly that God will work in their hearts to change them, and (2) we must lovingly confront them so as to "restore" them.

Some of you may be hurting right now from the pain of a prodigal son or daughter who has left the faith. Your child is beyond the confronting stage. All your attempts to restore him have only driven him further away from you and the Lord. You have prayed for years for your child and, as far as you can see, the Lord has not answered you a word. With the Canaanite woman you have cried out, "Lord, help me!" and no help has come. Well, pray on! Don't take no for a final answer when it comes to the salvation of your children. Be like Jacob—willing to struggle with God until He blesses you (Gen. 32:24-32). Be like the Canaanite moth-

er—humble yourself before the Lord (Matt. 15:27) and reason with Him until He says to you, "Your faith is great; be it
done for you as you wish" (v. 28).

There are many Christian parents who have seen God
answer their persevering prayers for a wayward son or
daughter. I know of one godly couple whose oldest son
planned to go into the ministry after he obtained his college and seminary training, but by the end of his first year
of college he had completely turned away from the Christian faith. For many years it looked as though he was going
to be a true casualty to the "wisdom of this world." But his
parents, along with many of us who knew and loved him,
continued to pray for his restoration. Some fifteen years
later, God answered our prayers. Today, this former *faith-
rejecter* is raising three children of his own with the goal of
leading them to know and serve God all of their days. So,
parents, learn to pray perseveringly.

PRAY TRUSTINGLY

Have you ever wondered why the Bible contains so many
stories of children whom God miraculously delivered from
Satan's control or raised from the dead? We can only spec-
ulate as to why the Holy Spirit focused on those two kinds
of deliverance. But these accounts assure us that God is
able to do the impossible when it comes to our children. If
He can deliver children from the clutches of Satan and
from the jaws of the grave prior to Christ's death and res-
urrection, then He most certainly can bring into His kingdom children who, though dead in trespasses and sin, are
living within the sphere of Gospel influence. The question
is, are we parents really willing to trust God with the eternal welfare of our children?

In Mark 9 we read about Christ healing a demon-
possessed child. The father had already taken his son to
Jesus' disciples, but they could not cast out the demon
(v. 18). Finally, in desperation, he calls out to Jesus, "If You
can do anything, take pity on us and help us!" (v. 22) Jesus

challenges the father's faith by responding, "'If You can!'
All things are possible to him who believes" (v. 23). The
man's honest reply was simply, "I do believe; help my unbelief" (v. 24).

Obviously, this man's confidence in Christ was not as
strong as the Canaanite woman's faith. Jesus said to her:
"O woman, your faith is great." This father's faith needed
some encouraging from the Lord. And yet, in both in-
stances, God honored their expressions of faith. Whether
weak faith or mighty faith, it was directed to the right
source. They both trusted in the power and mercy of Jesus
to deal graciously with the needs of their children. Is your
ultimate trust in Him alone?

Most of us, I'm afraid, bring our children to the Lord with
the attitude of this father, rather than with the faith of the
Canaanite mother. We come saying, "If You can do anything with my child, please do it. I believe in You, and yet I
still have doubts." We pray for our children's conversion,
all the while secretly fearing that maybe God won't save
them. We pray that He will help them overcome a particular sinful form of behavior, but deep down we wonder if He
really will. We believe, but we doubt too.

When my own faith is weak, I have often discovered a
discernible cause for my doubt. Sometimes it is the result
of unconfessed sin in my life. Because I am feeling guilty
over the sin, I am convinced God will not hear me when I
pray. Scripture seems to confirm this fact. (See Psalm
66:18, Mark 11:24-26, and 1 John 3:22.) True faith searches
the heart and leads to the confession of sin; it sanctifies the
pray-er and makes him ready to enter the holy of holies
with confidence. If we want to pray effectually for our
children, therefore, we must constantly examine our own
lives for sin that would grieve the Holy Spirit and impede
His blessing.

Another hindrance to praying in faith is not praying in
accordance with God's will (1 John 5:14). If God has given
us a clear promise in His Word, then we can pray in accor-

dance with that promise and trust God to keep it. In matters where God's will is not specifically revealed, we must first make sure our motives are honoring to Him and then boldly make our request (James 4:2-3; Heb. 4:16). We can always fully rest on two promises when we are praying without clear direction: (1) we can believe His promise that He will always do what is best for us and our children (Rom. 8:28; Matt. 7:7-11); (2) we can trust His promise through David that, if we find our greatest delight in Him and in His will, He will give us the desires of our heart (Ps. 37:4).

The bottom line to all of this is that God can be trusted with our children. But we must do the trusting. When Jesus' disciples asked Him why they could not cast out a demon, He replied, "This kind cannot come out by anything but prayer" (Mark 9:29). Praying in faith (i.e., a life characterized by prayer) is essential when it comes to rescuing the souls of our children from the evil one. We must practice the first twelve faith-formation principles with great diligence, but unless we pray with equal diligence, our parenting efforts will lack the divine energizing we all desire.

On one occasion, a Jewish ruler came to Jesus asking Him to heal his sick daughter. Before Jesus could arrive at the man's home, word arrived that the girl had died. You can imagine the agonized thoughts of the father as he heard the news: "Oh no, we're too late. I've lost her because I didn't seek Jesus sooner. If only I had been more insistent that He hurry. . . ." Parents are very good at blaming themselves when their children forsake the faith. And, unfortunately, sometimes parents are to blame. But notice what Jesus said to this grieving father. He said, "Do not be afraid any longer; only believe, and she shall be made well [literally saved]" (Luke 8:50).

One challenge I would like to leave with you as we draw this chapter and this study to a close, is the same message Jesus gave to this father who thought he was too late to save his girl: "Do not be afraid any longer; only believe, and your child shall be saved."

As you have considered these thirteen principles, you probably found yourself feeling somewhat overwhelmed. I did. Maybe you even feel intimidated by all that God expects of you as a Christian parent, or you have felt a twinge of guilt regarding some area where you know you have already failed to measure up to His standards of faith-formation. Do not be afraid. Do not despair. Our God is a God of forgiveness (1 John 1:9). He is a Father of mercy who understands our weaknesses (Ps. 103:13-14). He is not some sinister, mean ogre who delights in torturing us with doubts about whether our children will come to faith in Him. On the contrary, He tells us that He delights to give us good gifts (Matt. 7:7-11; James 1:17).

This most certainly includes the gift of our children. The psalmist specifically states that they are given as an inheritance and a blessing, not as a source of anguish (Ps. 127:3-5). God has also assured us that our children are special objects of His saving interest (Acts 2:39; 1 Cor. 7:14). What more need He say? Surely it is up to us now to *really believe* His Word and to teach, model, and pray accordingly. We don't have to fear; only believe.

PASS ON THE FAITH

Jesus once asked His disciples, "When the Son of Man comes, will He find faith on the earth?" (Luke 18:8) The faith that He was speaking about was the kind that leads men "at all times . . . to pray and not to lose heart" (Luke 18:1). I believe the answer to Jesus' question is a resounding "Yes!" Yes, there will be this kind of faith on the earth at Christ's second coming. As Christian parents, however, our immediate concern is: Will this kind of faith be found in the next generation? Will it be found in *our* children and in *our* children's children?

I believe it will. God will remain true to His promises. He will continue to draw the vast majority of His people from the line of generations. But we also must remain true to our parental calling. We must faithfully apply the faith-formation principles, and we must constantly water our efforts by praying redemptively, perseveringly, and trust-ingly, asking God to save and keep our children. Let us determine, therefore, that with God's help, "We will not conceal them from our children, but tell to the generation to come the praises of the Lord, and His strength and His wondrous works that He has done" (Ps. 78:4).

With these words, the psalmist describes the highest calling on earth—passing on the faith to the next genera-tion. In this book, I have tried to provide Christian parents with the help and incentives they need to be true to this calling. If it has accomplished that goal in your life, I urge you to dedicate yourself afresh to fulfilling the joyous privi-lege of leading your children to an enduring faith in Jesus Christ.

For Review, Discussion, and Action:

1. Reread the previous twelve faith-formation principles listed at the beginning of each chapter. In a few words list the essential truth of each principle. How do you feel after you list all the responsibilities God has placed on you? Now read the faith-formation principle for chapter 13. Why is this final principle so important?

2. What two responsibilities do we, like the prophet Sam-uel, have as parents toward our children? (See 1 Samuel 12:23-24.)

3. Define and illustrate from Scripture each of the follow-ing: (1) praying redemptively, (2) praying perseveringly, and (3) praying trustingly. On a scale of 1-10 (*1* meaning "rarely," *5* meaning "occasionally," and *10* meaning "regu-larly"), rate yourself in regard to each of these three char-acteristics of prayer.

4. Read, prayerfully consider, and then sign the following pledge:

> Realizing that God has called me to pass on to my children the true faith once delivered to the saints and that He holds me accountable for the truths I have learned from the study of these thirteen faith-formation principles, I hereby dedicate myself, with God's help, to diligently apply these principles to the rearing of my children.

Signature _____

Date _____

For Further Study:

Christenson, Larry. *The Christian Family*. Minneapolis: Bethany House Publishers, 1970. At points Christenson tends to be highly mystical in his description of praying for our children; however, his comments on prayer (chapter 7, "The Priesthood of Believers") are generally very helpful and practical.

Miller, John C. and Barbara Juliani. *Come Back, Barbara*. Grand Rapids: Zondervan Publishing House, 1988. For parents who are hurting over their child's rejection of the faith, this book holds the most promise of giving hope and direction. The central theme of chapter 3 is the role of prayer for one's wayward child.

Murray, Andrew. *How to Raise Your Children for Christ*. Minneapolis: Bethany Fellowship, Inc., 1975. In several chapters, Murray deals with the responsibility of parents to pray for their children, basing his observations on parents in the Scriptures who brought their children to Jesus for healing. In particular see chapters 11, 20, 29, 32, and 38.

Ray, Bruce A. *Withhold Not Correction.* Phillipsburg: Presbyterian and Reformed Publishing Company, 1978. The author has written a brief chapter (chapter 5) on praying as it relates to the area of child discipline.

Stanley, Charles. *How to Keep Your Kids on Your Team.* Nashville: Oliver Nelson Publishers, 1986. Dr. Stanley, in chapter 8, covers the broad subject of how to teach your children the importance of prayer.

NOTES

CHAPTER ONE: BEGIN WITH A CLEAR VIEW

1. Archibald Alexander, *Thoughts on Religious Experience* (London: The Banner of Truth Trust, 1844), p. 13.

2. Jay E. Adams, *Back to the Blackboard* (Phillipsburg: Presbyterian and Reformed Publishing Company, 1982) p. 60.

CHAPTER THREE: INCULCATE AND INOCULATE

1. Jay E. Adams, *Back to the Blackboard* (Phillipsburg: Presbyterian and Reformed Publishing Company, 1982), p. 104.

2. For a suggested model of faith development in children, based on the metaphor of physically healthy children, see the author's Doctor of Ministry Dissertation, *Parents Passing On the Faith*, Westminster Theological Seminary Library, 1988.

3. Bonnidell Clouse, *Moral Development: Perspectives in Psychology and Christian Belief* (Grand Rapids: Baker Book House, 1985), p. 340.

4. In a survey of seventh- and eighth-graders in one Christian school, the following results were recorded. Out of 48 students taking the survey, 45 had more than one TV set in their house, and 25 said they had a TV in their own bedroom. Forty said they had VCRs while 36 said their parents do not restrict their TV watching.

CHAPTER FOUR: KEEP THEM FROM THE EVIL ONE

1. For a more complete description of the various meanings of the term *world* as found in Johannine writings, see William Hendricksen, *New Testament Commentary: Exposition of the Gospel of John* (Grand Rapids: Baker Book House), 1953, p. 79.

2. John White, *Flirting with the World* (Wheaton: Harold Shaw Publishers), 1982, p. 23.

3. Ibid.

CHAPTER FIVE: AIM FOR THE HEART

1. For a deeply moving account of the painful struggles experienced by both Barbara and her parents during her rejection of and return to the faith, read *Come Back, Barbara* by John C. Miller and Barbara Miller Juliani (Grand Rapids: Zondervan Publishing House, 1988).

2. Most religious educators, influenced by the research of developmental psychologists like Jean Piaget and Ronald Goldman, would agree with the following comment: "A child's attitude is far more significant and enduring than his level of understanding information. Error in knowledge

can be corrected far more easily than negative feelings can be changed. Obviously the two areas are closely related and each has an influence upon the other. However, early in life the extreme limits of the child's reasoning abilities make emotional qualities more vital than at other stages of his development." Wes Haystead, *Teaching Your Child about God*, (Ventura: Regal Books, 1974), p. 131.

3. For discussions on the subject of self-image or self-esteem in our children see:
   Haystead, *Teaching Your Child about God*, pp. 29–52.
   Merton P. Strommen, *Five Cries of Youth* (San Francisco: Harper & Row, 1974), pp. 12–32.

4. From Flavel's *Saint Indeed* as quoted in Charles Bridges, *An Exposition of Proverbs* (Marshallton: The National Foundation for Christian Education), p. 53.

CHAPTER SIX: CREATE A CLIMATE OF UNCONDITIONAL LOVE

1. Ross Campbell, *How to Really Love Your Child* (Wheaton: Victor Books, 1977), p. 128.

2. Charles Stanley, *How to Keep Your Kids on Your Team* (Nashville: Oliver Nelson Publishers, 1986), p. 55.

CHAPTER EIGHT: BUILD UP, DON'T TEAR DOWN

1. Merton P. Strommen, *Five Cries of Youth* (New York: Harper & Row, 1979), p. xvi.

2. See, for example, Jay Adams, *The Christian Counselor's Manual* (Phillipsburg: Presbyterian and Reformed Publishing Company, 1973), pp. 141–47.

3. Strommen, *Five Cries of Youth*, p. 16.

4. Fritz Ridenour, *What Teenagers Wish Their Parents Knew about Kids*, Waco: Word Books, 1982), pp. 81–90.

5. Ibid., p. 83.

6. Ibid., p. 88.

CHAPTER NINE: COMMUNICATE A MESSAGE OF TRUST

1. I'm not sure where the term *deparent* originated, but Fritz Ridenour, in his book, *What Teenagers Wish Their Parents Knew about Kids*, refers to a helpful "Plan for Deparenting" as devised by Gary J. Hess. See Ridenour, p. 52.

CHAPTER TEN: PROVOKE NOT TO WRATH

1. Charles Barclay, *Letters to the Galatians and Ephesians* in the *Daily Study Bible* (The Saint Andrew Press, 1954), quoted in John R.W. Stott, *God's New Society* (Downers Grove: InterVarsity Press, 1979), p. 245.

2. Ronald P. Hutchcraft, "Life as a Single Parent," *Parents and Teenagers*, ed. Jay Kesler (Wheaton: Victor Books, 1984), p. 470.

3. Robert G. Barnes, *Single Parenting: A Wilderness Journey* (Wheaton: Tyndale House Publishers, 1984), p. 9.

4. Merton P. Strommen, *Five Cries of Youth* (New York: Harper & Row, 1979), p. 33.

5. For an excellent treatment of the meaning of the word *nouthesia*, see Jay Adams, *Competent to Counsel* (Phillipsburg: Presbyterian and Reformed Publishing Company, 1970), pp. 41–50.

6. John R.W. Stott, *God's New Society: The Message of Ephesians* (Downers Grove: InterVarsity Press, 1979), pp. 249–50.

CHAPTER ELEVEN: BE FAIR BUT BE FIRM

1. Fritz Ridenour, *What Teenagers Wish Their Parents Knew about Kids* (Waco: Word Books, 1982), p. 130.

2. For an interesting study comparing the dictatorial and authoritative styles of parenting as they affect attitudes of youth toward religion, see Roger Louis Dudley, "Alienation from Religion in Adolescents from Fundamentalist Religious Homes," *Journal for the Scientific Study of Religion*, Vol. 17, No. 4 (1978), pp. 389–98. Dudley's research fully supports the assumption that children raised by dictatorial parents are more likely to become alienated from their parents' faith than those raised by authoritative parents.

3. For example, Dr. Ross Campbell argues that we should first request a certain behavior of our child, then we should issue a command, and not until there is open defiance should we consider punishment. He writes, "Let's face it, corporal punishment is sometimes necessary to break a pronounced, belligerent defiance, but only as a last resort." Campbell, *How to Really Love Your Child* (Wheaton: Victor Books, 1977), p. 110.

4. Paul D. Meier, *Christian Child-Rearing and Personality Development* (Grand Rapids: Baker Book House, 1977), pp. 85-86.

5. Campbell, *How to Really Love Your Child*, p. 107.

6. This does not mean we must adopt the theories of behavior modification. They are based on a totally different set of presuppositions and, apart from their inclusion of

rewards and punishments, have very little in keeping with Christianity.

CHAPTER TWELVE: MODEL THE "LIGHT LOAD"

1. Reginald W. Bibby and Donald C. Posterski, *The Emerging Generation: An Inside Look at Canada's Teenagers* (Toronto: Irwin Publishing, 1985), p. 32.

2. Merton P. Strommen, *Five Cries of Youth* (New York: Harper & Row, 1979), p. 92.

3. Virginia Hearn, ed., *What They Did Right* (Wheaton: Tyndale House Publishers, 1974), p. 96.

4. Strommen, *Five Cries of Youth*, p. 53.

5. Ibid.

6. Fowler's developmental theory focuses on the six specific stages of human faith (not saving faith) as it progresses from infancy to adulthood. Much of what he says about faith in general, however, can be of tremendous help in understanding the mechanics or characteristics of faith at each given stage. For a brief description and critique of Fowler's stages of faith see the author's Doctor of Ministry thesis, *Parents Passing On the Faith*, Westminster Theological Seminary Library, 1988.

7. James W. Fowler, *Stages of Faith* (New York: Harper & Row, 1981), p. 182.

8. Strommen, *Five Cries of Youth*, p. 84.

9. Merton and Irene Strommen, "Raising Christian Children," *The Church Herald* (May 17, 1985), p. 14.

10. Fundamentalists Anonymous is an organization whose sole purpose is to support those who have left the fundamentalist branch of the church. Dr. Richard Yao, founder of FA informed me in May 1987 that the organization had a membership of 35,000 with an average of 200 inquiries for help a week. When asked what he thought were the primary reasons for young people raised in Christian homes rejecting the Christian faith he said, "The mindsets, rigidity, guilt-causing and discrimination against women and minorities."

CHAPTER THIRTEEN: PRAY! PRAY! PRAY!

1. Andrew Murray, *How to Raise Your Children for Christ* (Minneapolis: Bethany Fellowship Inc., 1975), p. 114.